TEACHER'S PET PUBLICATIONS

PUZZLE PACK
for
Brave New World
based on the book by
Aldous Huxley

Written by
William T. Collins

© 2005 Teacher's Pet Publications
All Rights Reserved

The materials in this packet are copyrighted
by Teacher's Pet Publications, Inc.

These pages may be duplicated by the purchaser
for use in the purchaser's own classroom.

Copying any of these materials and distributing them
for any other purpose is a violation of the copyright laws.

© 2005 Teacher's Pet Publications, Inc.
www.tpet.com

INTRODUCTION

If you already own the LitPlan for this title, this Puzzle Pack will refresh your Unit Resource Materials and Vocabulary Resource Materials sections plus give you additional materials you can substitute into the tests. If you do not already have a complete LitPlan, these pages will give you some supplemental materials to use with your own plan. There are two main groups of materials: one set for unit words (such as characters' names, symbols, places, etc.) and one set for vocabulary words associated with the book.

WORD LIST

There is a word list for both the unit words and the vocabulary words. These lists show you which words are being used in the materials and the clues or definitions being used for those words. You may want to give students a word list with clues/definitions to help them, or you may want students to only have a word list (without clues/definitions) if you want them to work a little harder. Both are available for duplication. The word lists can also be your "calling key" for the bingo games.

FILL IN THE BLANK AND MATCHING

There are 4 each of the fill in the blank and matching worksheets for both the unit and vocabulary words. These pages can be used either as extra worksheets for students or as objective parts of a unit test. They can be done individually if students need extra help or as a whole class activity to review the material covered.

MAGIC SQUARES

The magic squares not only reinforce the material covered but also work on reasoning and math skills. Many teachers have told us that their students really enjoy doing these!

WORD SEARCH PUZZLES

The word search words go in all directions, as indicated on your answer keys. Two of the word search puzzles have the clues listed rather than the words. This makes the puzzle a little more difficult, but it reinforces the material better. Two word search puzzles have words only for students who find the clue puzzles too difficult.

CROSSWORD PUZZLES

Both unit and vocabulary word sections have 4 crossword puzzles.

BINGO CARDS

There are 32 individual bingo cards for the unit words and 32 individual bingo cards for the vocabulary words. You can use your word list as a "call list," calling the words at random and marking them off of your list as you go, or you could use the flash cards by cutting them apart and drawing the words at random from a hat (or box or whatever). To make a better review, you might ask for the definition and spelling of each word as you call it out–or you could call out the definitions and have students tell you the words they need to look for on the puzzle.

JUGGLE LETTERS

The vocabulary juggle letter game is intended to help students learn the spellings of the words. One sheet has the definitions listed on it as an extra help for students who need it or to reinforce the definitions if you choose to do so.

FLASH CARDS

We've included a set of vocabulary flash cards you can duplicate, cut, and fold for your students. Some teachers make a few sets for general use by the class; others make a set for each student. Some teachers duplicate them for each student and have the students cut & fold their own. You can cut out just the words and put them in a hat, have each student pick out one word and write the definition and a sentence for that word. Students then swap words and papers, with the next student adding a sentence of his own under the last one. You can have students swap as many times as you like. Each time the student will read the sentences written prior to his own and then add a sentence. You can cut out the words and definitions separately and play "I Have; Who Has?" Each student in the room draws a word and definition. The first student says, "I have (the name of the word). Who has the definition?" The student with the definition reads it then says, "I have (the name of the vocabulary word she has). Who has the definition?" The round continues until all words and definitions have been given.

Brave New World Word List

No.	Word	Clue/Definition
1.	ALPHA	____ Plus; highest caste
2.	BOKANOVSKY	____'s Process makes multiple 'twin' embryos
3.	BOOKS	Babies were conditioned to hate these and flowers
4.	BOTTLE	There ain't no ____ in the world/Like that dear little ____ of mine.
5.	BRAVE	____New World
6.	CLAIM	I ____ them all!
7.	COMMUNITY	World State's motto: ____, Identity, Stability
8.	CONDITIONING	Director of Hatcheries and ____
9.	DEATH	Was considered something pleasant in the new world
10.	DELTAS	They do not need books to perform their social functions
11.	DESTINY	The point of conditioning is to make people like their inescapable social--
12.	DIRECTOR	John's father
13.	FEELIES	Movies
14.	FORD	Name of the deity in this world
15.	HANGS	John ____ himself.
16.	HATCHERIES	Director of ____ and Conditioning
17.	HELMHOLTZ	He realized that, like Bernard, he was an individual
18.	HUXLEY	Author
19.	IDENTICAL	____ workers at ____ machines will perform ____ tasks
20.	ISLAND	Place where Bernard was sent with most interesting people in the world
21.	JOHN	Linda's son
22.	JULIET	John compared Lenina to her
23.	LENINA	She went with Bernard to see the Savage Reservation
24.	LINDA	Beta who was lost during a visit to the Savage Reservation
25.	MALPAIS	Place where John was born
26.	MARX	Bernard's last name
27.	MITSIMA	He taught John how to work clay & make a bow
28.	MOTHER	An obscene word from the past
29.	NINE	When science first began to be controlled--after the ____ Years War.
30.	ODD	Lenina decided Bernard was ____
31.	POPE	He brought John The Complete Works of William Shakespeare
32.	PORGY	Orgy-____
33.	RESERVATION	Place where Linda and John lived
34.	SOCIAL	No civilization without ____stability, No ____ stability without individual stability.
35.	SOLIDARITY	____ Service is a religious type service where people take soma, chant & feel a oneness
36.	SOMA	Recreational, stress-relieving drug
37.	TREATS	Children were given these when visiting the hospital for the dying

Brave New World Fill In The Blanks 1

_____

_____

_____

_____

_____

_____

_____

_____

_____

_____

_____

_____

_____

_____

_____

_____

_____

_____

_____

_____

1. He brought John The Complete Works of William Shakespeare
2. Place where Linda and John lived
3. Place where John was born
4. ____New World
5. Place where Bernard was sent with most interesting people in the world
6. Bernard's last name
7. ____'s Process makes multiple 'twin' embryos
8. The point of conditioning is to make people like their inescapable social--
9. Director of Hatcheries and ____
10. She went with Bernard to see the Savage Reservation
11. Beta who was lost during a visit to the Savage Reservation
12. Babies were conditioned to hate these and flowers
13. John compared Lenina to her
14. ___ workers at ____ machines will perform ____ tasks
15. He taught John how to work clay & make a bow
16. Movies
17. Children were given these when visiting the hospital for the dying
18. I ____ them all!
19. John's father
20. World State's motto: ____, Identity, Stability

Brave New World Fill In The Blanks 1 Answer Key

POPE	1. He brought John The Complete Works of William Shakespeare
RESERVATION	2. Place where Linda and John lived
MALPAIS	3. Place where John was born
BRAVE	4. ____ New World
ISLAND	5. Place where Bernard was sent with most interesting people in the world
MARX	6. Bernard's last name
BOKANOVSKY	7. ____'s Process makes multiple 'twin' embryos
DESTINY	8. The point of conditioning is to make people like their inescapable social--
CONDITIONING	9. Director of Hatcheries and ____
LENINA	10. She went with Bernard to see the Savage Reservation
LINDA	11. Beta who was lost during a visit to the Savage Reservation
BOOKS	12. Babies were conditioned to hate these and flowers
JULIET	13. John compared Lenina to her
IDENTICAL	14. ____ workers at ____ machines will perform ____ tasks
MITSIMA	15. He taught John how to work clay & make a bow
FEELIES	16. Movies
TREATS	17. Children were given these when visiting the hospital for the dying
CLAIM	18. I ____ them all!
DIRECTOR	19. John's father
COMMUNITY	20. World State's motto: ____, Identity, Stability

Brave New World Fill In The Blanks 2

_____

_____

_____

_____

_____

_____

_____

_____

_____

_____

_____

_____

_____

_____

_____

_____

_____

_____

_____

_____

1. Author
2. Director of Hatcheries and ____
3. When science first began to be controlled--after the ____ Years War.
4. Place where Linda and John lived
5. No civilization without ____ stability, No ____ stability without individual stability.
6. Place where Bernard was sent with most interesting people in the world
7. He taught John how to work clay & make a bow
8. ____ New World
9. Babies were conditioned to hate these and flowers
10. They do not need books to perform their social functions
11. Director of ____ and Conditioning
12. Name of the deity in this world
13. Bernard's last name
14. John ____ himself.
15. He brought John The Complete Works of William Shakespeare
16. Linda's son
17. I ____ them all!
18. He realized that, like Bernard, he was an individual
19. John's father
20. ___ workers at ____ machines will perform ____ tasks

Brave New World Fill In The Blanks 2 Answer Key

HUXLEY	1. Author
CONDITIONING	2. Director of Hatcheries and ____
NINE	3. When science first began to be controlled--after the ____ Years War.
RESERVATION	4. Place where Linda and John lived
SOCIAL	5. No civilization without ____ stability, No ____ stability without individual stability.
ISLAND	6. Place where Bernard was sent with most interesting people in the world
MITSIMA	7. He taught John how to work clay & make a bow
BRAVE	8. ____ New World
BOOKS	9. Babies were conditioned to hate these and flowers
DELTAS	10. They do not need books to perform their social functions
HATCHERIES	11. Director of ____ and Conditioning
FORD	12. Name of the deity in this world
MARX	13. Bernard's last name
HANGS	14. John ____ himself.
POPE	15. He brought John The Complete Works of William Shakespeare
JOHN	16. Linda's son
CLAIM	17. I ____ them all!
HELMHOLTZ	18. He realized that, like Bernard, he was an individual
DIRECTOR	19. John's father
IDENTICAL	20. ___ workers at ____ machines will perform ____ tasks

Copyrighted

Brave New World Fill In The Blanks 3

_____

_____

_____

_____

_____

_____

_____

_____

_____

_____

_____

_____

_____

_____

_____

_____

_____

_____

_____

_____

1. Babies were conditioned to hate these and flowers
2. Linda's son
3. ___ workers at ____ machines will perform ____ tasks
4. Children were given these when visiting the hospital for the dying
5. There ain't no ____ in the world/Like that dear little ____ of mine.
6. Was considered something pleasant in the new world
7. Recreational, stress-relieving drug
8. Lenina decided Bernard was ____
9. He taught John how to work clay & make a bow
10. Director of Hatcheries and ____
11. Place where Linda and John lived
12. ____ Plus; highest caste
13. Movies
14. He realized that, like Bernard, he was an individual
15. John's father
16. John compared Lenina to her
17. ____ Service is a religious type service where people take soma, chant & feel a oneness
18. He brought John The Complete Works of William Shakespeare
19. Author
20. Beta who was lost during a visit to the Savage Reservation

Brave New World Fill In The Blanks 3 Answer Key

BOOKS	1. Babies were conditioned to hate these and flowers
JOHN	2. Linda's son
IDENTICAL	3. ___ workers at ____ machines will perform ____ tasks
TREATS	4. Children were given these when visiting the hospital for the dying
BOTTLE	5. There ain't no ____ in the world/Like that dear little ____ of mine.
DEATH	6. Was considered something pleasant in the new world
SOMA	7. Recreational, stress-relieving drug
ODD	8. Lenina decided Bernard was ____
MITSIMA	9. He taught John how to work clay & make a bow
CONDITIONING	10. Director of Hatcheries and ____
RESERVATION	11. Place where Linda and John lived
ALPHA	12. ____ Plus; highest caste
FEELIES	13. Movies
HELMHOLTZ	14. He realized that, like Bernard, he was an individual
DIRECTOR	15. John's father
JULIET	16. John compared Lenina to her
SOLIDARITY	17. ____ Service is a religious type service where people take soma, chant & feel a oneness
POPE	18. He brought John The Complete Works of William Shakespeare
HUXLEY	19. Author
LINDA	20. Beta who was lost during a visit to the Savage Reservation

Brave New World Fill In The Blanks 4

1. John ____ himself.
2. ____ Plus; highest caste
3. Director of ____ and Conditioning
4. Lenina decided Bernard was ____
5. Movies
6. She went with Bernard to see the Savage Reservation
7. ____ Service is a religious type service where people take soma, chant & feel a oneness
8. Beta who was lost during a visit to the Savage Reservation
9. World State's motto: ____, Identity, Stability
10. Orgy-____
11. He taught John how to work clay & make a bow
12. Place where Bernard was sent with most interesting people in the world
13. Linda's son
14. John's father
15. ____ New World
16. Babies were conditioned to hate these and flowers
17. He realized that, like Bernard, he was an individual
18. Recreational, stress-relieving drug
19. Children were given these when visiting the hospital for the dying
20. An obscene word from the past

Brave New World Fill In The Blanks 4 Answer Key

HANGS	1. John ____ himself.
ALPHA	2. ____ Plus; highest caste
HATCHERIES	3. Director of ____ and Conditioning
ODD	4. Lenina decided Bernard was ____
FEELIES	5. Movies
LENINA	6. She went with Bernard to see the Savage Reservation
SOLIDARITY	7. ____ Service is a religious type service where people take soma, chant & feel a oneness
LINDA	8. Beta who was lost during a visit to the Savage Reservation
COMMUNITY	9. World State's motto: ____, Identity, Stability
PORGY	10. Orgy-____
MITSIMA	11. He taught John how to work clay & make a bow
ISLAND	12. Place where Bernard was sent with most interesting people in the world
JOHN	13. Linda's son
DIRECTOR	14. John's father
BRAVE	15. ____ New World
BOOKS	16. Babies were conditioned to hate these and flowers
HELMHOLTZ	17. He realized that, like Bernard, he was an individual
SOMA	18. Recreational, stress-relieving drug
TREATS	19. Children were given these when visiting the hospital for the dying
MOTHER	20. An obscene word from the past

Brave New World Matching 1

___ 1. JOHN
___ 2. ALPHA
___ 3. DEATH
___ 4. ISLAND
___ 5. HANGS
___ 6. JULIET
___ 7. POPE
___ 8. ODD
___ 9. SOMA
___ 10. SOCIAL
___ 11. CLAIM
___ 12. SOLIDARITY
___ 13. CONDITIONING
___ 14. MOTHER
___ 15. COMMUNITY
___ 16. LENINA
___ 17. LINDA
___ 18. DELTAS
___ 19. BRAVE
___ 20. FORD
___ 21. HATCHERIES
___ 22. HUXLEY
___ 23. MALPAIS
___ 24. BOKANOVSKY
___ 25. HELMHOLTZ

A. Author
B. John ____ himself.
C. ____ Plus; highest caste
D. World State's motto: ____, Identity, Stability
E. Recreational, stress-relieving drug
F. Name of the deity in this world
G. No civilization without ____ stability, No ____ stability without individual stability.
H. He realized that, like Bernard, he was an individual
I. Director of Hatcheries and ____
J. ____ Service is a religious type service where people take soma, chant & feel a oneness
K. Beta who was lost during a visit to the Savage Reservation
L. He brought John The Complete Works of William Shakespeare
M. Place where Bernard was sent with most interesting people in the world
N. Director of ____ and Conditioning
O. John compared Lenina to her
P. An obscene word from the past
Q. Place where John was born
R. Was considered something pleasant in the new world
S. She went with Bernard to see the Savage Reservation
T. ____ New World
U. I ____ them all!
V. Lenina decided Bernard was ____
W. ____'s Process makes multiple 'twin' embryos
X. They do not need books to perform their social functions
Y. Linda's son

Brave New World Matching 1 Answer Key

Y - 1. JOHN
C - 2. ALPHA
R - 3. DEATH
M - 4. ISLAND
B - 5. HANGS
O - 6. JULIET
L - 7. POPE
V - 8. ODD
E - 9. SOMA
G - 10. SOCIAL
U - 11. CLAIM
J - 12. SOLIDARITY
I - 13. CONDITIONING
P - 14. MOTHER
D - 15. COMMUNITY
S - 16. LENINA
K - 17. LINDA
X - 18. DELTAS
T - 19. BRAVE
F - 20. FORD
N - 21. HATCHERIES
A - 22. HUXLEY
Q - 23. MALPAIS
W - 24. BOKANOVSKY
H - 25. HELMHOLTZ

A. Author
B. John ____ himself.
C. ____ Plus; highest caste
D. World State's motto: ____, Identity, Stability
E. Recreational, stress-relieving drug
F. Name of the deity in this world
G. No civilization without ____ stability, No ____ stability without individual stability.
H. He realized that, like Bernard, he was an individual
I. Director of Hatcheries and ____
J. ____ Service is a religious type service where people take soma, chant & feel a oneness
K. Beta who was lost during a visit to the Savage Reservation
L. He brought John The Complete Works of William Shakespeare
M. Place where Bernard was sent with most interesting people in the world
N. Director of ____ and Conditioning
O. John compared Lenina to her
P. An obscene word from the past
Q. Place where John was born
R. Was considered something pleasant in the new world
S. She went with Bernard to see the Savage Reservation
T. ____ New World
U. I ____ them all!
V. Lenina decided Bernard was ____
W. ____'s Process makes multiple 'twin' embryos
X. They do not need books to perform their social functions
Y. Linda's son

Brave New World Matching 2

___ 1. TREATS A. John's father
___ 2. HELMHOLTZ B. Place where Linda and John lived
___ 3. DEATH C. Children were given these when visiting the hospital for the dying
___ 4. BOOKS D. He brought John The Complete Works of William Shakespeare
___ 5. RESERVATION E. Babies were conditioned to hate these and flowers
___ 6. DIRECTOR F. No civilization without ____ stability, No ____ stability without individual stability.
___ 7. FORD G. The point of conditioning is to make people like their inescapable social--
___ 8. HUXLEY H. He realized that, like Bernard, he was an individual
___ 9. POPE I. ____ Plus; highest caste
___ 10. MOTHER J. I ____ them all!
___ 11. FEELIES K. An obscene word from the past
___ 12. BOTTLE L. He taught John how to work clay & make a bow
___ 13. LENINA M. Author
___ 14. CLAIM N. She went with Bernard to see the Savage Reservation
___ 15. HATCHERIES O. There ain't no ____ in the world/Like that dear little ____ of mine.
___ 16. CONDITIONING P. Movies
___ 17. JOHN Q. Lenina decided Bernard was ____
___ 18. SOCIAL R. Place where Bernard was sent with most interesting people in the world
___ 19. DESTINY S. Name of the deity in this world
___ 20. MITSIMA T. Director of Hatcheries and ____
___ 21. SOMA U. Recreational, stress-relieving drug
___ 22. ALPHA V. ____'s Process makes multiple 'twin' embryos
___ 23. ODD W. Linda's son
___ 24. ISLAND X. Was considered something pleasant in the new world
___ 25. BOKANOVSKY Y. Director of ____ and Conditioning

Brave New World Matching 2 Answer Key

C - 1. TREATS
H - 2. HELMHOLTZ
X - 3. DEATH
E - 4. BOOKS
B - 5. RESERVATION
A - 6. DIRECTOR
S - 7. FORD
M - 8. HUXLEY
D - 9. POPE
K - 10. MOTHER
P - 11. FEELIES
O - 12. BOTTLE
N - 13. LENINA
J - 14. CLAIM
Y - 15. HATCHERIES
T - 16. CONDITIONING
W - 17. JOHN
F - 18. SOCIAL
G - 19. DESTINY
L - 20. MITSIMA
U - 21. SOMA
I - 22. ALPHA
Q - 23. ODD
R - 24. ISLAND
V - 25. BOKANOVSKY

A. John's father
B. Place where Linda and John lived
C. Children were given these when visiting the hospital for the dying
D. He brought John The Complete Works of William Shakespeare
E. Babies were conditioned to hate these and flowers
F. No civilization without ____ stability, No ____ stability without individual stability.
G. The point of conditioning is to make people like their inescapable social--
H. He realized that, like Bernard, he was an individual
I. ____ Plus; highest caste
J. I ____ them all!
K. An obscene word from the past
L. He taught John how to work clay & make a bow
M. Author
N. She went with Bernard to see the Savage Reservation
O. There ain't no ____ in the world/Like that dear little ____ of mine.
P. Movies
Q. Lenina decided Bernard was ____
R. Place where Bernard was sent with most interesting people in the world
S. Name of the deity in this world
T. Director of Hatcheries and ____
U. Recreational, stress-relieving drug
V. ____'s Process makes multiple 'twin' embryos
W. Linda's son
X. Was considered something pleasant in the new world
Y. Director of ____ and Conditioning

Brave New World Matching 3

___ 1. ALPHA
___ 2. BOKANOVSKY
___ 3. COMMUNITY
___ 4. DELTAS
___ 5. NINE
___ 6. DESTINY
___ 7. BOOKS
___ 8. RESERVATION
___ 9. MITSIMA
___ 10. IDENTICAL
___ 11. HELMHOLTZ
___ 12. SOCIAL
___ 13. DEATH
___ 14. JOHN
___ 15. MOTHER
___ 16. POPE
___ 17. HATCHERIES
___ 18. BRAVE
___ 19. TREATS
___ 20. CONDITIONING
___ 21. PORGY
___ 22. ODD
___ 23. CLAIM
___ 24. ISLAND
___ 25. FEELIES

A. Orgy-____
B. ____'s Process makes multiple 'twin' embryos
C. Children were given these when visiting the hospital for the dying
D. He taught John how to work clay & make a bow
E. Babies were conditioned to hate these and flowers
F. They do not need books to perform their social functions
G. No civilization without ____ stability, No ____ stability without individual stability.
H. I ____ them all!
I. He realized that, like Bernard, he was an individual
J. The point of conditioning is to make people like their inescapable social--
K. Was considered something pleasant in the new world
L. ____ Plus; highest caste
M. When science first began to be controlled--after the ____ Years War.
N. ___ workers at ____ machines will perform ____ tasks
O. Lenina decided Bernard was ____
P. An obscene word from the past
Q. ____ New World
R. Director of ____ and Conditioning
S. He brought John The Complete Works of William Shakespeare
T. Movies
U. Place where Linda and John lived
V. Place where Bernard was sent with most interesting people in the world
W. Director of Hatcheries and ____
X. World State's motto: ____, Identity, Stability
Y. Linda's son

Brave New World Matching 3 Answer Key

L - 1. ALPHA
B - 2. BOKANOVSKY
X - 3. COMMUNITY
F - 4. DELTAS
M - 5. NINE
J - 6. DESTINY
E - 7. BOOKS
U - 8. RESERVATION
D - 9. MITSIMA
N - 10. IDENTICAL
I - 11. HELMHOLTZ
G - 12. SOCIAL
K - 13. DEATH
Y - 14. JOHN
P - 15. MOTHER
S - 16. POPE
R - 17. HATCHERIES
Q - 18. BRAVE
C - 19. TREATS
W - 20. CONDITIONING
A - 21. PORGY
O - 22. ODD
H - 23. CLAIM
V - 24. ISLAND
T - 25. FEELIES

A. Orgy-____
B. ____'s Process makes multiple 'twin' embryos
C. Children were given these when visiting the hospital for the dying
D. He taught John how to work clay & make a bow
E. Babies were conditioned to hate these and flowers
F. They do not need books to perform their social functions
G. No civilization without ____ stability, No ____ stability without individual stability.
H. I ____ them all!
I. He realized that, like Bernard, he was an individual
J. The point of conditioning is to make people like their inescapable social--
K. Was considered something pleasant in the new world
L. ____ Plus; highest caste
M. When science first began to be controlled--after the ____ Years War.
N. ___ workers at ____ machines will perform ____ tasks
O. Lenina decided Bernard was ____
P. An obscene word from the past
Q. ____ New World
R. Director of ____ and Conditioning
S. He brought John The Complete Works of William Shakespeare
T. Movies
U. Place where Linda and John lived
V. Place where Bernard was sent with most interesting people in the world
W. Director of Hatcheries and ____
X. World State's motto: ____, Identity, Stability
Y. Linda's son

Brave New World Matching 4

___ 1. DESTINY
___ 2. ODD
___ 3. CLAIM
___ 4. BOOKS
___ 5. SOMA
___ 6. MARX
___ 7. LINDA
___ 8. COMMUNITY
___ 9. POPE
___ 10. HANGS
___ 11. DELTAS
___ 12. HUXLEY
___ 13. RESERVATION
___ 14. IDENTICAL
___ 15. HATCHERIES
___ 16. MOTHER
___ 17. FEELIES
___ 18. CONDITIONING
___ 19. ISLAND
___ 20. DIRECTOR
___ 21. BOKANOVSKY
___ 22. MALPAIS
___ 23. BOTTLE
___ 24. MITSIMA
___ 25. BRAVE

A. World State's motto: ____, Identity, Stability
B. ____ New World
C. There ain't no ____ in the world/Like that dear little ____ of mine.
D. Director of ____ and Conditioning
E. Lenina decided Bernard was ____
F. An obscene word from the past
G. Bernard's last name
H. ____'s Process makes multiple 'twin' embryos
I. He taught John how to work clay & make a bow
J. Movies
K. Director of Hatcheries and ____
L. ___ workers at ____ machines will perform ____ tasks
M. The point of conditioning is to make people like their inescapable social--
N. Place where Bernard was sent with most interesting people in the world
O. Place where John was born
P. I ____ them all!
Q. Recreational, stress-relieving drug
R. They do not need books to perform their social functions
S. John's father
T. He brought John The Complete Works of William Shakespeare
U. Babies were conditioned to hate these and flowers
V. Author
W. John ____ himself.
X. Beta who was lost during a visit to the Savage Reservation
Y. Place where Linda and John lived

Brave New World Matching 4 Answer Key

M - 1. DESTINY	A.	World State's motto: ____, Identity, Stability
E - 2. ODD	B.	____ New World
P - 3. CLAIM	C.	There ain't no ____ in the world/Like that dear little ____ of mine.
U - 4. BOOKS	D.	Director of ____ and Conditioning
Q - 5. SOMA	E.	Lenina decided Bernard was ____
G - 6. MARX	F.	An obscene word from the past
X - 7. LINDA	G.	Bernard's last name
A - 8. COMMUNITY	H.	____'s Process makes multiple 'twin' embryos
T - 9. POPE	I.	He taught John how to work clay & make a bow
W -10. HANGS	J.	Movies
R -11. DELTAS	K.	Director of Hatcheries and ____
V -12. HUXLEY	L.	___ workers at ____ machines will perform ____ tasks
Y -13. RESERVATION	M.	The point of conditioning is to make people like their inescapable social--
L -14. IDENTICAL	N.	Place where Bernard was sent with most interesting people in the world
D -15. HATCHERIES	O.	Place where John was born
F -16. MOTHER	P.	I ____ them all!
J -17. FEELIES	Q.	Recreational, stress-relieving drug
K -18. CONDITIONING	R.	They do not need books to perform their social functions
N -19. ISLAND	S.	John's father
S -20. DIRECTOR	T.	He brought John The Complete Works of William Shakespeare
H -21. BOKANOVSKY	U.	Babies were conditioned to hate these and flowers
O -22. MALPAIS	V.	Author
C -23. BOTTLE	W.	John ____ himself.
I -24. MITSIMA	X.	Beta who was lost during a visit to the Savage Reservation
B -25. BRAVE	Y.	Place where Linda and John lived

Brave New World Magic Squares 1

Match the definition with the vocabulary word. Put your answers in the magic squares below. When your answers are correct, all columns and rows will add to the same number.

A. LENINA
B. SOMA
C. HUXLEY
D. BRAVE
E. MARX
F. BOOKS
G. BOTTLE
H. TREATS
I. DEATH
J. JULIET
K. ISLAND
L. ODD
M. COMMUNITY
N. CONDITIONING
O. FORD
P. JOHN

1. Children were given these when visiting the hospital for the dying
2. She went with Bernard to see the Savage Reservation
3. Recreational, stress-relieving drug
4. There ain't no ____ in the world/Like that dear little ____ of mine.
5. John compared Lenina to her
6. Name of the deity in this world
7. Linda's son
8. Was considered something pleasant in the new world
9. Place where Bernard was sent with most interesting people in the world
10. Director of Hatcheries and ____
11. World State's motto: ____, Identity, Stability
12. Lenina decided Bernard was ____
13. Bernard's last name
14. ____ New World
15. Author
16. Babies were conditioned to hate these and flowers

A=	B=	C=	D=
E=	F=	G=	H=
I=	J=	K=	L=
M=	N=	O=	P=

Brave New World Magic Squares 1 Answer Key

Match the definition with the vocabulary word. Put your answers in the magic squares below. When your answers are correct, all columns and rows will add to the same number.

A. LENINA
B. SOMA
C. HUXLEY
D. BRAVE
E. MARX
F. BOOKS
G. BOTTLE
H. TREATS
I. DEATH
J. JULIET
K. ISLAND
L. ODD
M. COMMUNITY
N. CONDITIONING
O. FORD
P. JOHN

1. Children were given these when visiting the hospital for the dying
2. She went with Bernard to see the Savage Reservation
3. Recreational, stress-relieving drug
4. There ain't no ____ in the world/Like that dear little ____ of mine.
5. John compared Lenina to her
6. Name of the deity in this world
7. Linda's son
8. Was considered something pleasant in the new world
9. Place where Bernard was sent with most interesting people in the world
10. Director of Hatcheries and ____
11. World State's motto: ____, Identity, Stability
12. Lenina decided Bernard was ____
13. Bernard's last name
14. ____ New World
15. Author
16. Babies were conditioned to hate these and flowers

A=2	B=3	C=15	D=14
E=13	F=16	G=4	H=1
I=8	J=5	K=9	L=12
M=11	N=10	O=6	P=7

Brave New World Magic Squares 2

Match the definition with the vocabulary word. Put your answers in the magic squares below. When your answers are correct, all columns and rows will add to the same number.

A. MITSIMA
B. BOTTLE
C. NINE
D. ALPHA
E. DELTAS
F. PORGY
G. CLAIM
H. IDENTICAL
I. JULIET
J. DIRECTOR
K. HANGS
L. LINDA
M. DESTINY
N. CONDITIONING
O. MALPAIS
P. SOMA

1. Orgy-____
2. John compared Lenina to her
3. Place where John was born
4. ____ Plus; highest caste
5. The point of conditioning is to make people like their inescapable social--
6. There ain't no ____ in the world/Like that dear little ____ of mine.
7. ___ workers at ____ machines will perform ____ tasks
8. John ____ himself.
9. When science first began to be controlled--after the ____ Years War.
10. Recreational, stress-relieving drug
11. John's father
12. They do not need books to perform their social functions
13. Beta who was lost during a visit to the Savage Reservation
14. I ____ them all!
15. He taught John how to work clay & make a bow
16. Director of Hatcheries and ____

A=	B=	C=	D=
E=	F=	G=	H=
I=	J=	K=	L=
M=	N=	O=	P=

Brave New World Magic Squares 2 Answer Key

Match the definition with the vocabulary word. Put your answers in the magic squares below. When your answers are correct, all columns and rows will add to the same number.

A. MITSIMA
B. BOTTLE
C. NINE
D. ALPHA
E. DELTAS
F. PORGY
G. CLAIM
H. IDENTICAL
I. JULIET
J. DIRECTOR
K. HANGS
L. LINDA
M. DESTINY
N. CONDITIONING
O. MALPAIS
P. SOMA

1. Orgy-____
2. John compared Lenina to her
3. Place where John was born
4. ____ Plus; highest caste
5. The point of conditioning is to make people like their inescapable social--
6. There ain't no ____ in the world/Like that dear little ____ of mine.
7. ___ workers at ____ machines will perform ____ tasks
8. John ____ himself.
9. When science first began to be controlled--after the ____ Years War.
10. Recreational, stress-relieving drug
11. John's father
12. They do not need books to perform their social functions
13. Beta who was lost during a visit to the Savage Reservation
14. I ____ them all!
15. He taught John how to work clay & make a bow
16. Director of Hatcheries and ____

A=15	B=6	C=9	D=4
E=12	F=1	G=14	H=7
I=2	J=11	K=8	L=13
M=5	N=16	O=3	P=10

Brave New World Magic Squares 3

Match the definition with the vocabulary word. Put your answers in the magic squares below. When your answers are correct, all columns and rows will add to the same number.

A. DESTINY
B. JOHN
C. MALPAIS
D. ISLAND
E. SOMA
F. ALPHA
G. TREATS
H. FORD
I. NINE
J. MITSIMA
K. POPE
L. CLAIM
M. BRAVE
N. PORGY
O. COMMUNITY
P. BOOKS

1. Name of the deity in this world
2. ____ New World
3. Linda's son
4. He brought John The Complete Works of William Shakespeare
5. He taught John how to work clay & make a bow
6. Place where John was born
7. Babies were conditioned to hate these and flowers
8. Recreational, stress-relieving drug
9. World State's motto: ____, Identity, Stability
10. ____ Plus; highest caste
11. When science first began to be controlled--after the ____ Years War.
12. Place where Bernard was sent with most interesting people in the world
13. The point of conditioning is to make people like their inescapable social--
14. I ____ them all!
15. Children were given these when visiting the hospital for the dying
16. Orgy-____

A=	B=	C=	D=
E=	F=	G=	H=
I=	J=	K=	L=
M=	N=	O=	P=

Brave New World Magic Squares 3 Answer Key

Match the definition with the vocabulary word. Put your answers in the magic squares below. When your answers are correct, all columns and rows will add to the same number.

A. DESTINY
B. JOHN
C. MALPAIS
D. ISLAND
E. SOMA
F. ALPHA
G. TREATS
H. FORD
I. NINE
J. MITSIMA
K. POPE
L. CLAIM
M. BRAVE
N. PORGY
O. COMMUNITY
P. BOOKS

1. Name of the deity in this world
2. ____New World
3. Linda's son
4. He brought John The Complete Works of William Shakespeare
5. He taught John how to work clay & make a bow
6. Place where John was born
7. Babies were conditioned to hate these and flowers
8. Recreational, stress-relieving drug
9. World State's motto: ____, Identity, Stability
10. ____ Plus; highest caste
11. When science first began to be controlled--after the ____ Years War.
12. Place where Bernard was sent with most interesting people in the world
13. The point of conditioning is to make people like their inescapable social--
14. I ____ them all!
15. Children were given these when visiting the hospital for the dying
16. Orgy-____

A=13	B=3	C=6	D=12
E=8	F=10	G=15	H=1
I=11	J=5	K=4	L=14
M=2	N=16	O=9	P=7

Brave New World Magic Squares 4

Match the definition with the vocabulary word. Put your answers in the magic squares below. When your answers are correct, all columns and rows will add to the same number.

A. SOCIAL
B. RESERVATION
C. DEATH
D. DIRECTOR
E. MITSIMA
F. BOOKS
G. FORD
H. NINE
I. CONDITIONING
J. BRAVE
K. ODD
L. ALPHA
M. LENINA
N. LINDA
O. POPE
P. DESTINY

1. She went with Bernard to see the Savage Reservation
2. Babies were conditioned to hate these and flowers
3. When science first began to be controlled--after the ____ Years War.
4. He brought John The Complete Works of William Shakespeare
5. ____ Plus; highest caste
6. Was considered something pleasant in the new world
7. No civilization without ____ stability, No ____ stability without individual stability.
8. ____ New World
9. Lenina decided Bernard was ____
10. John's father
11. Place where Linda and John lived
12. Director of Hatcheries and ____
13. Beta who was lost during a visit to the Savage Reservation
14. He taught John how to work clay & make a bow
15. Name of the deity in this world
16. The point of conditioning is to make people like their inescapable social--

A=	B=	C=	D=
E=	F=	G=	H=
I=	J=	K=	L=
M=	N=	O=	P=

Brave New World Magic Squares 4 Answer Key

Match the definition with the vocabulary word. Put your answers in the magic squares below. When your answers are correct, all columns and rows will add to the same number.

A. SOCIAL
B. RESERVATION
C. DEATH
D. DIRECTOR
E. MITSIMA
F. BOOKS
G. FORD
H. NINE
I. CONDITIONING
J. BRAVE
K. ODD
L. ALPHA
M. LENINA
N. LINDA
O. POPE
P. DESTINY

1. She went with Bernard to see the Savage Reservation
2. Babies were conditioned to hate these and flowers
3. When science first began to be controlled--after the ____ Years War.
4. He brought John The Complete Works of William Shakespeare
5. ____ Plus; highest caste
6. Was considered something pleasant in the new world
7. No civilization without ____stability, No ____ stability without individual stability.
8. ____New World
9. Lenina decided Bernard was ____
10. John's father
11. Place where Linda and John lived
12. Director of Hatcheries and ____
13. Beta who was lost during a visit to the Savage Reservation
14. He taught John how to work clay & make a bow
15. Name of the deity in this world
16. The point of conditioning is to make people like their inescapable social--

A=7	B=11	C=6	D=10
E=14	F=2	G=15	H=3
I=12	J=8	K=9	L=5
M=1	N=13	O=4	P=16

Brave New World Word Search 1

Words are placed backwards, forward, diagonally, up and down. Clues listed below can help you find the words. Circle the hidden vocabulary words in the maze.

```
C O N D I T I O N I N G T S F T P T K
B O K A N O V S K Y X L X Z H Y L K S
H E L M H O L T Z Q Z C Q A T Y R V P
R E S E R V A T I O N C T I F M Y K S
T B S V M L Y F N H W C N X L V L P F
B R O H V Q N V J F H U P H K S D P W
L S F T N B I Y M E M H T A L B C X Q
I Z E G T C T J R M G I B N Q I S R J
X S E L Q L S I O D Y M T G P T N M D
D E L T A S E C T R E A T S O M A D D
N P I A Y S D S S O Z A I H I W O J A
W O E V N S G S O F H A T P H M V U C
H P S S J D M P C C P U G H N L A L J
D I R E C T O R I L B M X N I N E I P
V P B D F R T F A A E R A L Y W T E D
P H Z O G C H M L I D N A R E F M T L
D M X Y O J E C L M W X I V X Y Q L R
J O H N V K R W V X Q X G N E P P V S
L S L K H L S I D E N T I C A L P H A
```

An obscene word from the past (6)
Author (6)
Babies were conditioned to hate these and flowers (5)
Bernard's last name (4)
Beta who was lost during a visit to the Savage Reservation (5)
Children were given these when visiting the hospital for the dying (6)
Director of Hatcheries and ____ (12)
Director of ____ and Conditioning (10)
He brought John The Complete Works of William Shakespeare (4)
He realized that, like Bernard, he was an individual (9)
He taught John how to work clay & make a bow (7)
I ____ them all! (5)
John ____ himself. (5)
John compared Lenina to her (6)
John's father (8)
Lenina decided Bernard was ____ (3)
Linda's son (4)
Movies (7)
Name of the deity in this world (4)
No civilization without ____ stability, No ____ stability without individual stability. (6)
Orgy-____ (5)
Place where Bernard was sent with most interesting people in the world (6)
Place where John was born (7)
Place where Linda and John lived (11)
Recreational, stress-relieving drug (4)
She went with Bernard to see the Savage Reservation (6)
The point of conditioning is to make people like their inescapable social-- (7)
There ain't no ____ in the world/Like that dear little ____ of mine. (6)
They do not need books to perform their social functions (6)
Was considered something pleasant in the new world (5)
When science first began to be controlled--after the ____ Years War. (4)
World State's motto: ____, Identity, Stability (9)
___ workers at ____ machines will perform ____ tasks (9)
____ Plus; highest caste (5)
____'s Process makes multiple 'twin' embryos (10)
____ New World (5)

Brave New World Word Search 1 Answer Key

Words are placed backwards, forward, diagonally, up and down. Clues listed below can help you find the words. Circle the hidden vocabulary words in the maze.

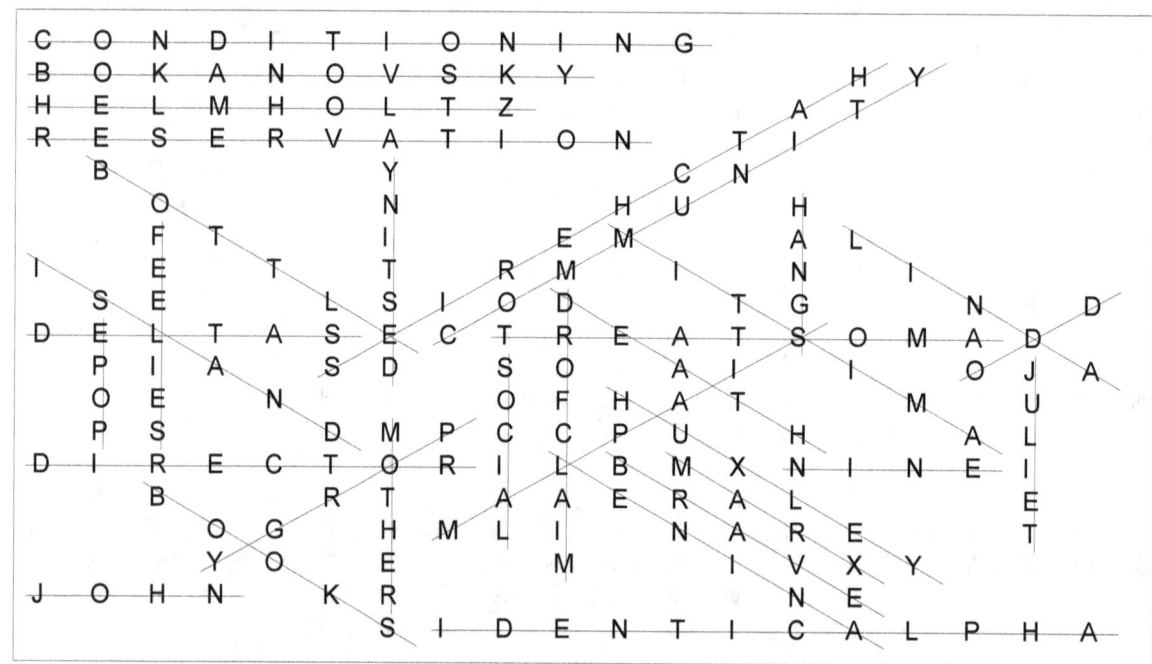

An obscene word from the past (6)
Author (6)
Babies were conditioned to hate these and flowers (5)
Bernard's last name (4)
Beta who was lost during a visit to the Savage Reservation (5)
Children were given these when visiting the hospital for the dying (6)
Director of Hatcheries and ____ (12)
Director of ____ and Conditioning (10)
He brought John The Complete Works of William Shakespeare (4)
He realized that, like Bernard, he was an individual (9)
He taught John how to work clay & make a bow (7)
I ____ them all! (5)
John ____ himself. (5)
John compared Lenina to her (6)
John's father (8)
Lenina decided Bernard was ____ (3)
Linda's son (4)
Movies (7)
Name of the deity in this world (4)
No civilization without ____stability, No ____ stability without individual stability. (6)
Orgy-____ (5)
Place where Bernard was sent with most interesting people in the world (6)
Place where John was born (7)
Place where Linda and John lived (11)
Recreational, stress-relieving drug (4)
She went with Bernard to see the Savage Reservation (6)
The point of conditioning is to make people like their inescapable social-- (7)
There ain't no ____ in the world/Like that dear little ____ of mine. (6)
They do not need books to perform their social functions (6)
Was considered something pleasant in the new world (5)
When science first began to be controlled--after the ____ Years War. (4)
World State's motto: ____, Identity, Stability (9)
___ workers at ____ machines will perform ____ tasks (9)
____ Plus; highest caste (5)
____'s Process makes multiple 'twin' embryos (10)
____New World (5)

Brave New World Word Search 2

Words are placed backwards, forward, diagonally, up and down. Clues listed below can help you find the words. Circle the hidden vocabulary words in the maze.

```
C O M M U N I T Y S Q S Q J N C N T P
G S N N H N M F Q D G T K O K J C C W
B O O K S I S L A N D R E H T O M B C
L Q I C M Y C N A P B E T N Q I R K Y
S H T W I C B H I F M A T R T A B Y R
N V A F V A X Y N N E T L S V B X K Y
R M V H U X L E Y D E S I E Y V E S V
B B R H D B A P F K E M K G N P K V P
L B E C E O C Z H H A S R B O I M O K
L L S J L T I X R A M O T P L Z N N N
T W E M T T T Q L T P M B I I P C A C
C V R T A L N F B C X A D G N T Q K M
X L S F S E E S E H X B B K D Y P O S
K G A Q Q D D I R E C T O R A S D B M
S K H I R J I A R R L K Q M N D M P F
X F J O M H W P Y I S I P H O B S T M
L K F P Y J U L I E T V E W K W M R L
J S Q K J R J A Y S C Q X S H V D B K
S L C F L B X M H E L M H O L T Z V Y
```

An obscene word from the past (6)
Author (6)
Babies were conditioned to hate these and flowers (5)
Bernard's last name (4)
Beta who was lost during a visit to the Savage Reservation (5)
Children were given these when visiting the hospital for the dying (6)
Director of ____ and Conditioning (10)
He brought John The Complete Works of William Shakespeare (4)
He realized that, like Bernard, he was an individual (9)
He taught John how to work clay & make a bow (7)
I ____ them all! (5)
John ____ himself. (5)
John compared Lenina to her (6)
John's father (8)
Lenina decided Bernard was ____ (3)
Linda's son (4)
Movies (7)
Name of the deity in this world (4)
No civilization without ____ stability, No ____ stability without individual stability. (6)

Orgy-____ (5)
Place where Bernard was sent with most interesting people in the world (6)
Place where John was born (7)
Place where Linda and John lived (11)
Recreational, stress-relieving drug (4)
She went with Bernard to see the Savage Reservation (6)
The point of conditioning is to make people like their inescapable social-- (7)
There ain't no ____ in the world/Like that dear little ____ of mine. (6)
They do not need books to perform their social functions (6)
Was considered something pleasant in the new world (5)
When science first began to be controlled--after the ____ Years War. (4)
World State's motto: ____, Identity, Stability (9)
___ workers at ____ machines will perform ____ tasks (9)
____ Plus; highest caste (5)
____'s Process makes multiple 'twin' embryos (10)
____ New World (5)

Brave New World Word Search 2 Answer Key

Words are placed backwards, forward, diagonally, up and down. Clues listed below can help you find the words. Circle the hidden vocabulary words in the maze.

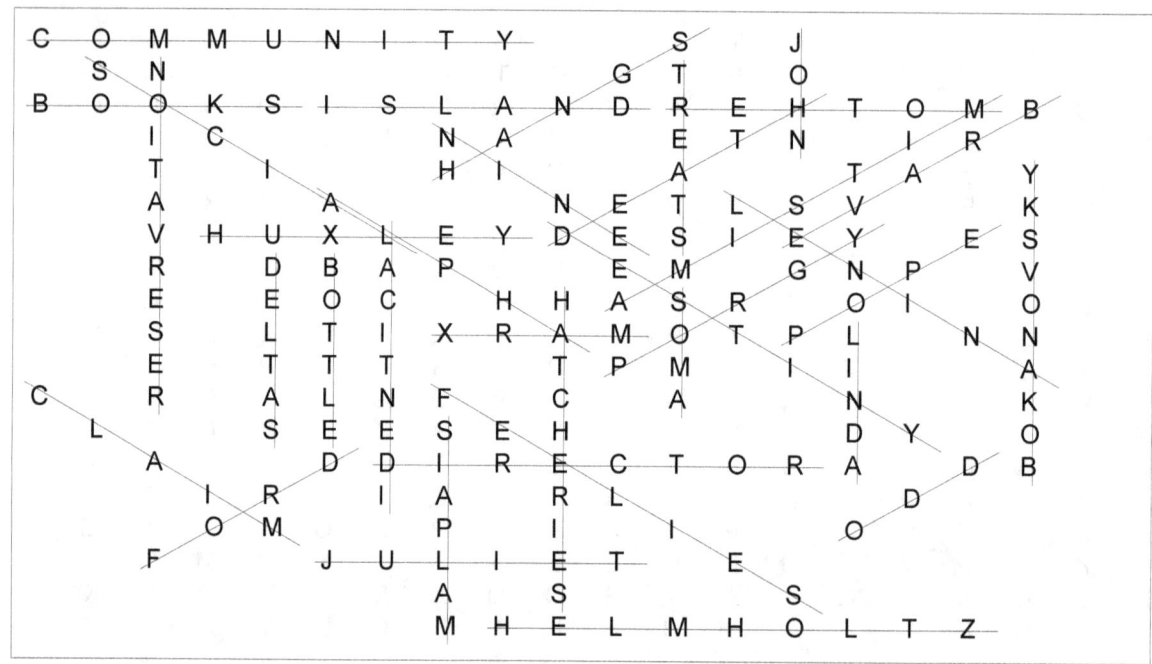

An obscene word from the past (6)
Author (6)
Babies were conditioned to hate these and flowers (5)
Bernard's last name (4)
Beta who was lost during a visit to the Savage Reservation (5)
Children were given these when visiting the hospital for the dying (6)
Director of ____ and Conditioning (10)
He brought John The Complete Works of William Shakespeare (4)
He realized that, like Bernard, he was an individual (9)
He taught John how to work clay & make a bow (7)
I ____ them all! (5)
John ____ himself. (5)
John compared Lenina to her (6)
John's father (8)
Lenina decided Bernard was ____ (3)
Linda's son (4)
Movies (7)
Name of the deity in this world (4)
No civilization without ____ stability, No ____ stability without individual stability. (6)

Orgy-____ (5)
Place where Bernard was sent with most interesting people in the world (6)
Place where John was born (7)
Place where Linda and John lived (11)
Recreational, stress-relieving drug (4)
She went with Bernard to see the Savage Reservation (6)
The point of conditioning is to make people like their inescapable social-- (7)
There ain't no ____ in the world/Like that dear little ____ of mine. (6)
They do not need books to perform their social functions (6)
Was considered something pleasant in the new world (5)
When science first began to be controlled--after the ____ Years War. (4)
World State's motto: ____, Identity, Stability (9)
___ workers at ____ machines will perform ____ tasks (9)
____ Plus; highest caste (5)
____'s Process makes multiple 'twin' embryos (10)
____ New World (5)

Brave New World Word Search 3

Words are placed backwards, forward, diagonally, up and down. Words listed below are included in the maze. Circle the hidden vocabulary words in the maze.

```
L X E N Y D B P Z S V C C Z B F C H R
A T P J I B Y T G K R R L B Y O O A S
N L O Z T N L S P O B S X A N R N N T
F H P D D O E S R O T C E R I D D G L
N E P H H Z T A T B R V H S T M I S J
H Q E M A A D T X P A G L M S H T D H
S Y L L E N L L K R G A Y A E A I E Y
C E Q R I E G E B Y N Y K R D T O A D
H O T L B E W D E D X N S X G C N T Q
K T M P E D S L X H J M V F G H I H R
J S J M B N X S O M A Y O V G E N Q T
P Z U Y U U I B Z P Q Y N T T R G X M
J G L X H N Q N V Q H Z A Z H I L V S
L A I C O S I J A S J R K J M E D J B
D Z E I D E N T I C A L O Y W S R F H
M C T Q T S H S Y P X B B V H M S X M
M A L P A I S W J B X Y R Z Q D F L T
M I T S I M A S O L I D A R I T Y X M
R E S E R V A T I O N G S J D Y G P M
```

ALPHA   DESTINY   JOHN   POPE

BOKANOVSKY   DIRECTOR   JULIET   PORGY

BOOKS   FEELIES   LENINA   RESERVATION

BOTTLE   FORD   LINDA   SOCIAL

BRAVE   HANGS   MALPAIS   SOLIDARITY

CLAIM   HATCHERIES   MARX   SOMA

COMMUNITY   HELMHOLTZ   MITSIMA   TREATS

CONDITIONING   HUXLEY   MOTHER

DEATH   IDENTICAL   NINE

DELTAS   ISLAND   ODD

33
Copyrighted

Brave New World Word Search 3 Answer Key

Words are placed backwards, forward, diagonally, up and down. Words listed below are included in the maze. Circle the hidden vocabulary words in the maze.

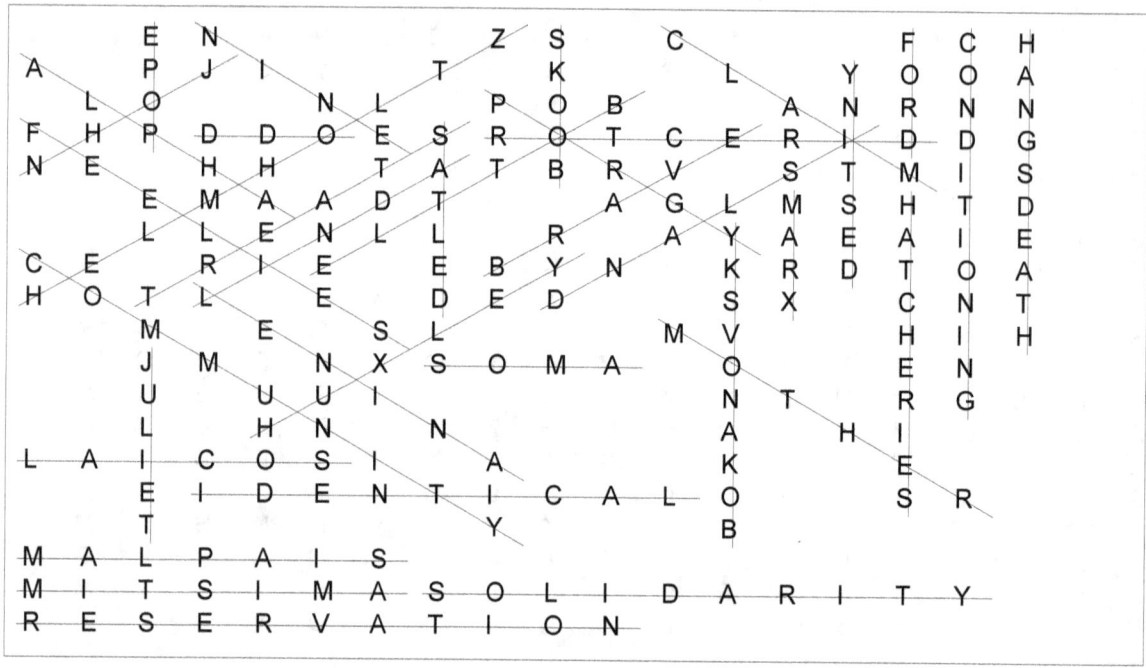

ALPHA	DESTINY	JOHN	POPE
BOKANOVSKY	DIRECTOR	JULIET	PORGY
BOOKS	FEELIES	LENINA	RESERVATION
BOTTLE	FORD	LINDA	SOCIAL
BRAVE	HANGS	MALPAIS	SOLIDARITY
CLAIM	HATCHERIES	MARX	SOMA
COMMUNITY	HELMHOLTZ	MITSIMA	TREATS
CONDITIONING	HUXLEY	MOTHER	
DEATH	IDENTICAL	NINE	
DELTAS	ISLAND	ODD	

Brave New World Word Search 4

Words are placed backwards, forward, diagonally, up and down. Words listed below are included in the maze. Circle the hidden vocabulary words in the maze.

```
H S I A P L A M L I N D A J U L I E T
A P P H N N L R D B F D Q G O S X L T L
T O L A I B M E W S D O M N L H H T M
C P K N N Y N I T S E D R A D T N T S
H E E G E T O Z T F G E N D A R G O S
E L P S I H I B D S H D G E F E M B C
R S L C H U T T O T I D D Y E A I C V
I O A D L X A Q O O D M G T E T A O M
E L I T L V M V O K R A I L S L N G
S I C G L E R D R Z O S B N I F C D H
M D O R C Y E I V P F G G U E J Y I M
A A S T Y G S R Y D P C J M S F Z T M
R R D Z X V E E X S L C D M A Z H I N
X I B E F S R C H E L M H O L T Z O B
M T R Q L Y D T N S Z H C P R D N Q
H Y A F P T N O X C Q R P V H D V I Q
B W V N K G A R M G P V Q J A Y H N Q
N R E J G L T S B N V J B H P V R G F
G G M J C G R T B O K A N O V S K Y Q
```

ALPHA	DESTINY	JOHN	POPE
BOKANOVSKY	DIRECTOR	JULIET	PORGY
BOOKS	FEELIES	LENINA	RESERVATION
BOTTLE	FORD	LINDA	SOCIAL
BRAVE	HANGS	MALPAIS	SOLIDARITY
CLAIM	HATCHERIES	MARX	SOMA
COMMUNITY	HELMHOLTZ	MITSIMA	TREATS
CONDITIONING	HUXLEY	MOTHER	
DEATH	IDENTICAL	NINE	
DELTAS	ISLAND	ODD	

Brave New World Word Search 4 Answer Key

Words are placed backwards, forward, diagonally, up and down. Words listed below are included in the maze. Circle the hidden vocabulary words in the maze.

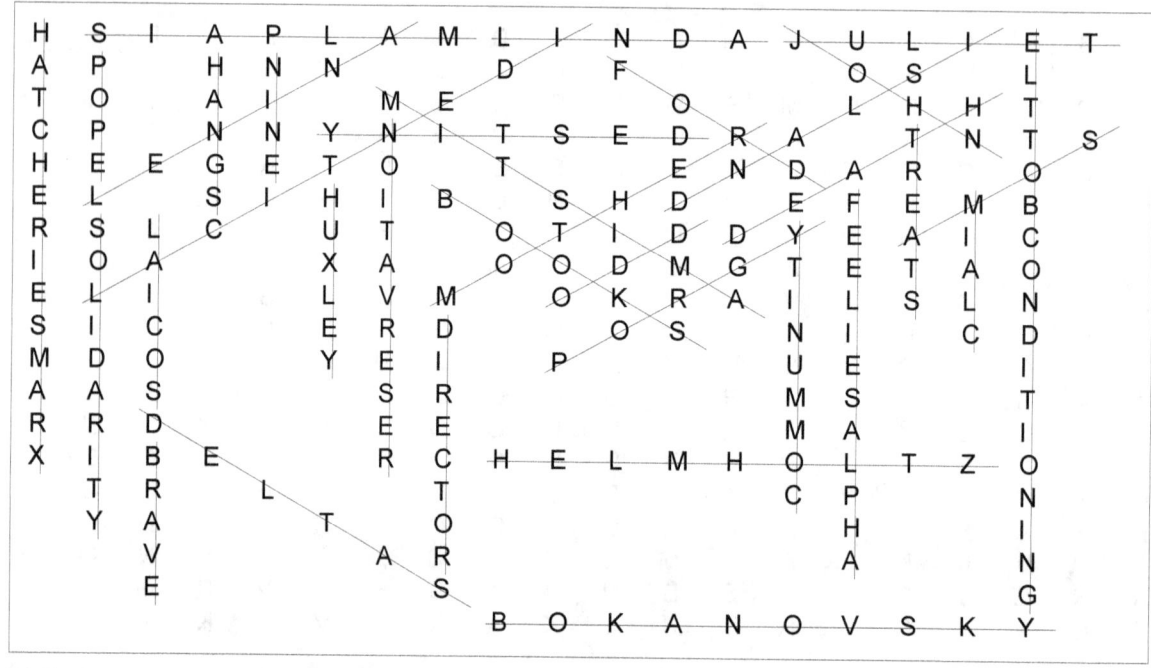

ALPHA	DESTINY	JOHN	POPE
BOKANOVSKY	DIRECTOR	JULIET	PORGY
BOOKS	FEELIES	LENINA	RESERVATION
BOTTLE	FORD	LINDA	SOCIAL
BRAVE	HANGS	MALPAIS	SOLIDARITY
CLAIM	HATCHERIES	MARX	SOMA
COMMUNITY	HELMHOLTZ	MITSIMA	TREATS
CONDITIONING	HUXLEY	MOTHER	
DEATH	IDENTICAL	NINE	
DELTAS	ISLAND	ODD	

Brave New World Crossword 1

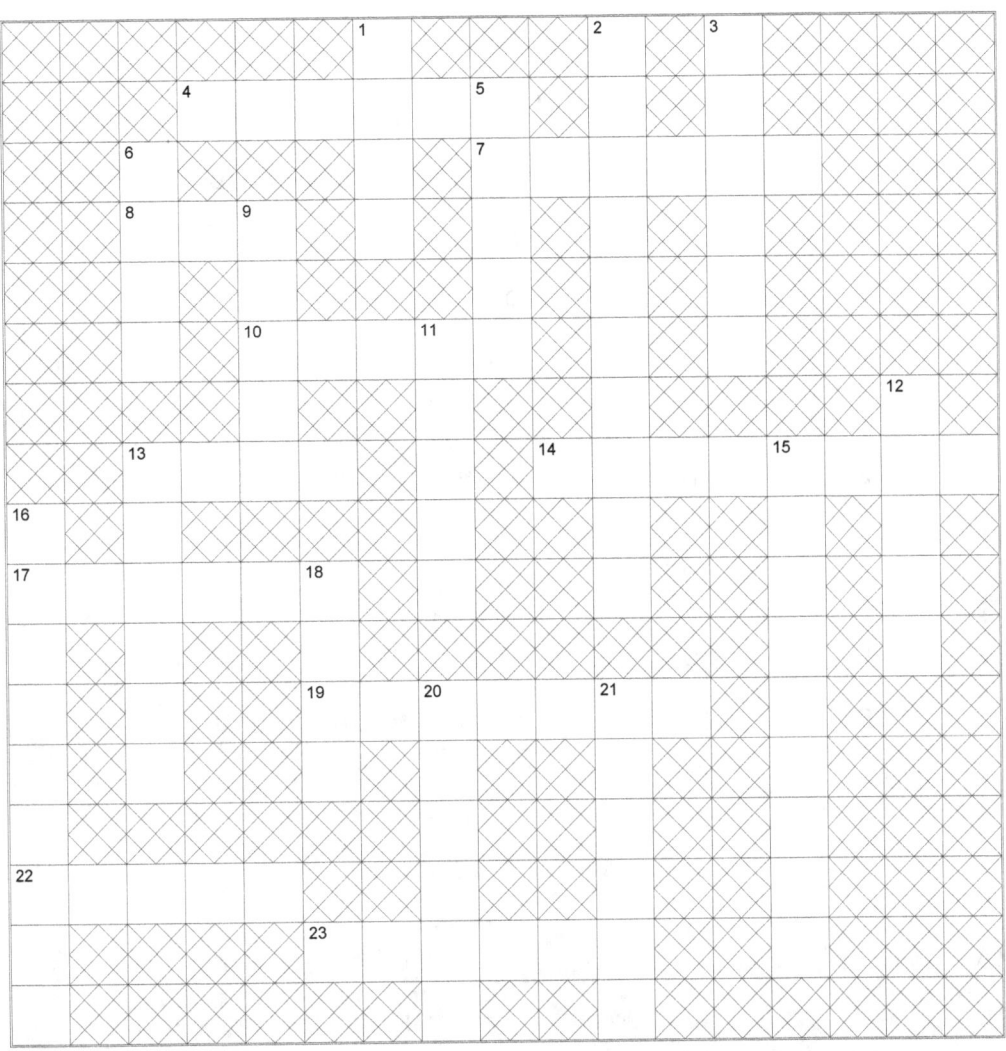

Across
4. No civilization without ____ stability, No ____ stability without individual stability.
7. Place where Bernard was sent with most interesting people in the world
8. Lenina decided Bernard was ____
10. ____ Plus; highest caste
13. Linda's son
14. John's father
17. They do not need books to perform their social functions
19. He taught John how to work clay & make a bow
22. I ____ them all!
23. There ain't no ____ in the world/Like that dear little ____ of mine.

Down
1. When science first began to be controlled--after the ____ Years War.
2. ____ Service is a religious type service where people take soma, chant & feel a oneness
3. She went with Bernard to see the Savage Reservation
5. Beta who was lost during a visit to the Savage Reservation
6. He brought John The Complete Works of William Shakespeare
9. Was considered something pleasant in the new world
11. John ____ himself.
12. Orgy-____
13. John compared Lenina to her
15. World State's motto: ____, Identity, Stability
16. ____ workers at ____ machines will perform ____ tasks
18. Recreational, stress-relieving drug
20. Children were given these when visiting the hospital for the dying
21. An obscene word from the past

Brave New World Crossword 1 Answer Key

Across

4. No civilization without ____ stability, No ____ stability without individual stability.
7. Place where Bernard was sent with most interesting people in the world
8. Lenina decided Bernard was ____
10. ____ Plus; highest caste
13. Linda's son
14. John's father
17. They do not need books to perform their social functions
19. He taught John how to work clay & make a bow
22. I ____ them all!
23. There ain't no ____ in the world/Like that dear little ____ of mine.

Down

1. When science first began to be controlled--after the ____ Years War.
2. ____ Service is a religious type service where people take soma, chant & feel a oneness
3. She went with Bernard to see the Savage Reservation
5. Beta who was lost during a visit to the Savage Reservation
6. He brought John The Complete Works of William Shakespeare
9. Was considered something pleasant in the new world
11. John ____ himself.
12. Orgy-____
13. John compared Lenina to her
15. World State's motto: ____, Identity, Stability
16. ___ workers at ____ machines will perform ____ tasks
18. Recreational, stress-relieving drug
20. Children were given these when visiting the hospital for the dying
21. An obscene word from the past

Brave New World Crossword 2

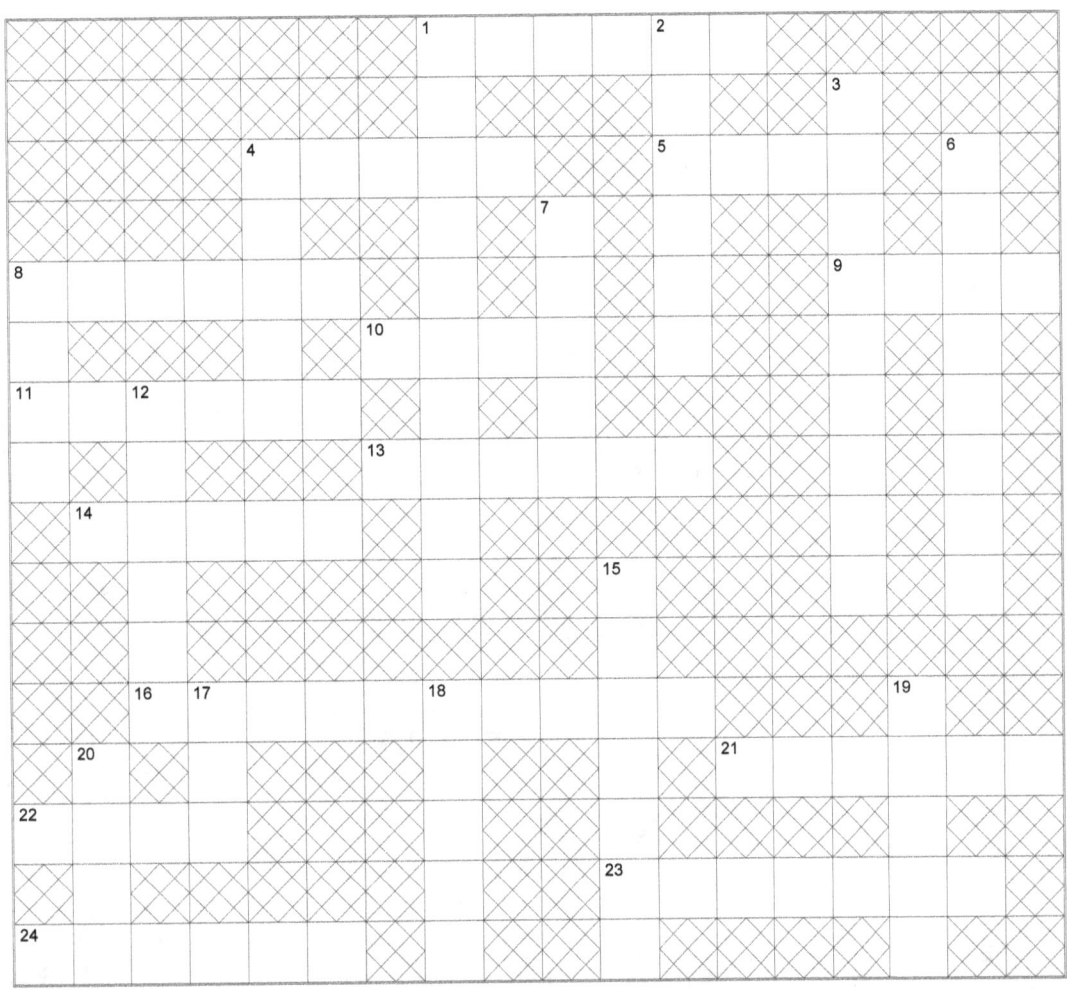

Across
1. There ain't no ____ in the world/Like that dear little ____ of mine.
4. Babies were conditioned to hate these and flowers
5. When science first began to be controlled--after the ____ Years War.
8. No civilization without ____stability, No ____ stability without individual stability.
9. Bernard's last name
10. Linda's son
11. An obscene word from the past
13. Place where Bernard was sent with most interesting people in the world
14. Was considered something pleasant in the new world
16. ____ Service is a religious type service where people take soma, chant & feel a oneness
21. Author
22. Name of the deity in this world
23. Place where John was born
24. They do not need books to perform their social functions

Down
1. ____'s Process makes multiple 'twin' embryos
2. She went with Bernard to see the Savage Reservation
3. He realized that, like Bernard, he was an individual
4. ____New World
6. John's father
7. Beta who was lost during a visit to the Savage Reservation
8. Recreational, stress-relieving drug
12. Children were given these when visiting the hospital for the dying
15. He taught John how to work clay & make a bow
17. Lenina decided Bernard was ____
18. ____ Plus; highest caste
19. I ____ them all!
20. He brought John The Complete Works of William Shakespeare

Brave New World Crossword 2 Answer Key

Across
1. There ain't no ____ in the world/Like that dear little ____ of mine.
4. Babies were conditioned to hate these and flowers
5. When science first began to be controlled--after the ____ Years War.
8. No civilization without ____ stability, No ____ stability without individual stability.
9. Bernard's last name
10. Linda's son
11. An obscene word from the past
13. Place where Bernard was sent with most interesting people in the world
14. Was considered something pleasant in the new world
16. ____ Service is a religious type service where people take soma, chant & feel a oneness
21. Author
22. Name of the deity in this world
23. Place where John was born
24. They do not need books to perform their social functions

Down
1. ____'s Process makes multiple 'twin' embryos
2. She went with Bernard to see the Savage Reservation
3. He realized that, like Bernard, he was an individual
4. ____ New World
6. John's father
7. Beta who was lost during a visit to the Savage Reservation
8. Recreational, stress-relieving drug
12. Children were given these when visiting the hospital for the dying
15. He taught John how to work clay & make a bow
17. Lenina decided Bernard was ____
18. ____ Plus; highest caste
19. I ____ them all!
20. He brought John The Complete Works of William Shakespeare

Brave New World Crossword 3

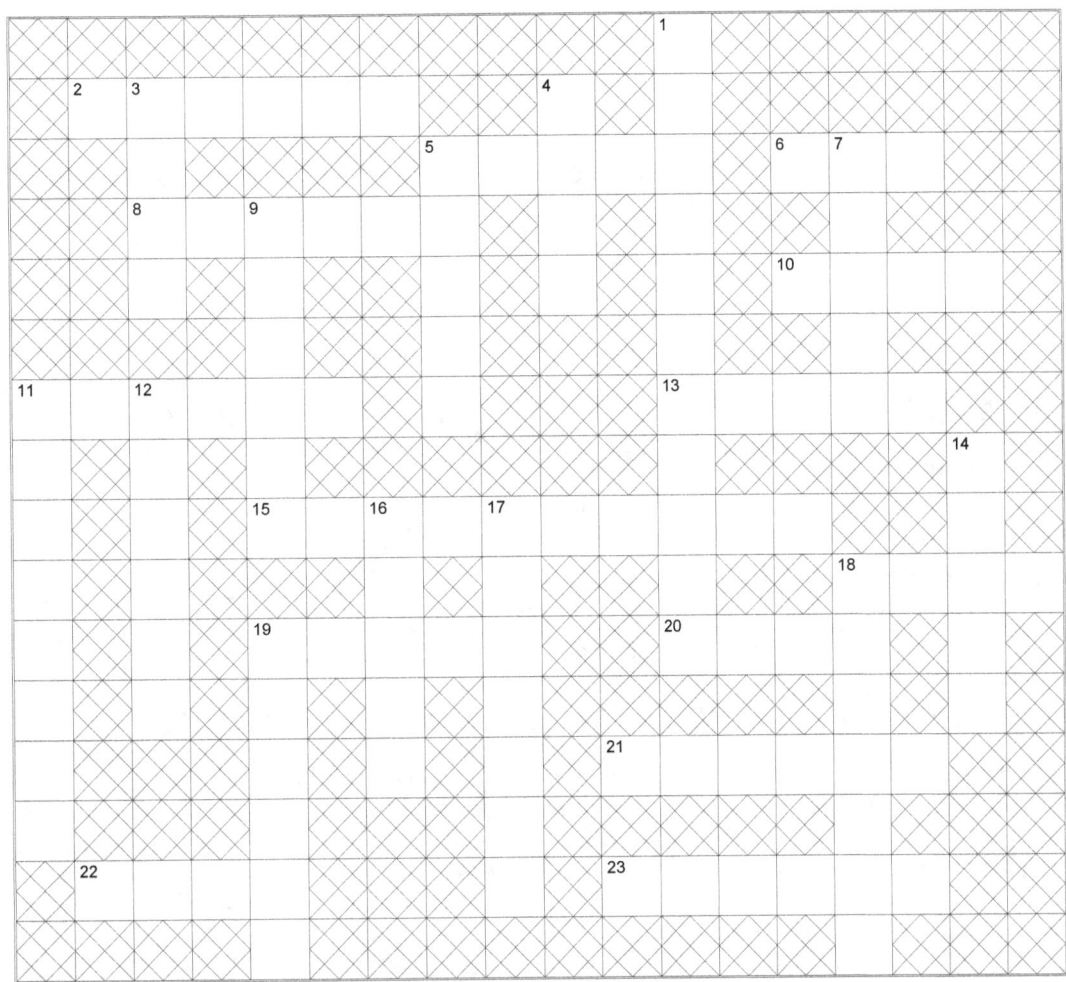

Across
2. Place where Bernard was sent with most interesting people in the world
5. Babies were conditioned to hate these and flowers
6. Lenina decided Bernard was ____
8. An obscene word from the past
10. Bernard's last name
11. They do not need books to perform their social functions
13. ____ Plus; highest caste
15. ____ Service is a religious type service where people take soma, chant & feel a oneness
18. Name of the deity in this world
19. John ____ himself.
20. When science first began to be controlled--after the ____ Years War.
21. There ain't no ____ in the world/Like that dear little ____ of mine.
22. He brought John The Complete Works of William Shakespeare
23. John compared Lenina to her

Down
1. Place where Linda and John lived
3. Recreational, stress-relieving drug
4. Linda's son
5. ____ New World
7. Was considered something pleasant in the new world
9. Children were given these when visiting the hospital for the dying
11. John's father
12. She went with Bernard to see the Savage Reservation
14. Orgy-____
16. Beta who was lost during a visit to the Savage Reservation
17. The point of conditioning is to make people like their inescapable social--
18. Movies
19. Author

Brave New World Crossword 3 Answer Key

		2 I	3 S	L	A	N	D		4 J	1 R E		6 O	7 D	D
			O			5 B	O	O	K	S			E	
		8 M	O	9 T	H	E	R		H	E		10 M	A	R X
			A	R		A			N	R		A	T	
				E		V				V		T		
11 D	E	L	12 T	A	S		E			13 A	L	P	H	A
I			E							T				14 P
R			N		15 S	16 O	L	17 I	D	A	R	I	T	Y	O
E			I			I		E		O			18 F	O	R	D
C			N		19 H	A	N	G	S		20 N	I	N	E
T			A		U			D			I		E		G
O					X			A		21 B	O	T	T	L	E
R					L			I					I		Y
		22 P	O	P	E			N		23 J	U	L	I	E	T
					Y									S	

Across

2. Place where Bernard was sent with most interesting people in the world
5. Babies were conditioned to hate these and flowers
6. Lenina decided Bernard was ____
8. An obscene word from the past
10. Bernard's last name
11. They do not need books to perform their social functions
13. ____ Plus; highest caste
15. ____ Service is a religious type service where people take soma, chant & feel a oneness
18. Name of the deity in this world
19. John ____ himself.
20. When science first began to be controlled--after the ____ Years War.
21. There ain't no ____ in the world/Like that dear little ____ of mine.
22. He brought John The Complete Works of William Shakespeare
23. John compared Lenina to her

Down

1. Place where Linda and John lived
3. Recreational, stress-relieving drug
4. Linda's son
5. ____ New World
7. Was considered something pleasant in the new world
9. Children were given these when visiting the hospital for the dying
11. John's father
12. She went with Bernard to see the Savage Reservation
14. Orgy-____
16. Beta who was lost during a visit to the Savage Reservation
17. The point of conditioning is to make people like their inescapable social--
18. Movies
19. Author

Brave New World Crossword 4

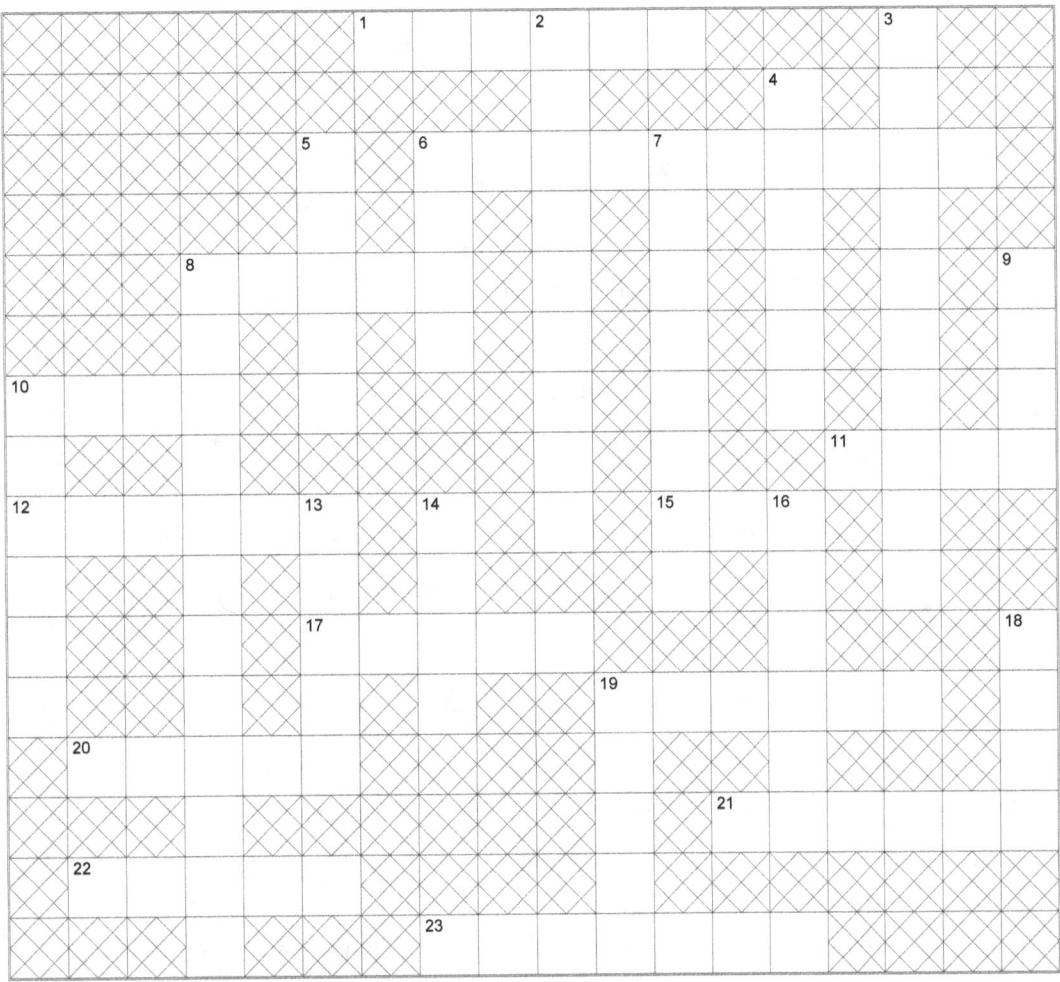

Across
1. An obscene word from the past
6. ____ Service is a religious type service where people take soma, chant & feel a oneness
8. I ____ them all!
10. Linda's son
11. When science first began to be controlled--after the ____ Years War.
12. She went with Bernard to see the Savage Reservation
15. Lenina decided Bernard was ____
17. Orgy-____
19. There ain't no ____ in the world/Like that dear little ____ of mine.
20. Beta who was lost during a visit to the Savage Reservation
21. Place where Bernard was sent with most interesting people in the world
22. John ____ himself.
23. He taught John how to work clay & make a bow

Down
2. He realized that, like Bernard, he was an individual
3. Director of ____ and Conditioning
4. Children were given these when visiting the hospital for the dying
5. ____ New World
6. Recreational, stress-relieving drug
7. John's father
8. Director of Hatcheries and ____
9. He brought John The Complete Works of William Shakespeare
10. John compared Lenina to her
13. ____ Plus; highest caste
14. Bernard's last name
16. They do not need books to perform their social functions
18. Name of the deity in this world
19. Babies were conditioned to hate these and flowers

Brave New World Crossword 4 Answer Key

					1 M	O	2 T H	H E	E R				3 H	
							E				4 T		A	
				5 B		6 S	O	L	I	7 D	A	R	I	T	Y
				R		O		M		I		E		C	
			8 C	L	A	I	M		H		R		A		H		9 P
			O		V		A		O		E		T		E		O
10 J	O	H	N		E				L		C		S		R		P
U			D						T		T			11 N	I	N	E
12 L	E	13 N	I	N	A		14 M		Z		15 O	D	16 D		E		
I		T			L		A				R		E		S		
E		I		17 P	O	R	G	Y					L				18 F
T		O		H			X		19 B	O	T	T	L	E			O
	20 L	I	N	D	A				O			A					R
		I						21 O		I	S	L	A	N	D
	22 H	A	N	G	S				K							
		G				23 M	I	T	S	I	M	A		

Across
1. An obscene word from the past
6. ____ Service is a religious type service where people take soma, chant & feel a oneness
8. I ____ them all!
10. Linda's son
11. When science first began to be controlled--after the ____ Years War.
12. She went with Bernard to see the Savage Reservation
15. Lenina decided Bernard was ____
17. Orgy-____
19. There ain't no ____ in the world/Like that dear little ____ of mine.
20. Beta who was lost during a visit to the Savage Reservation
21. Place where Bernard was sent with most interesting people in the world
22. John ____ himself.
23. He taught John how to work clay & make a bow

Down
2. He realized that, like Bernard, he was an individual
3. Director of ____ and Conditioning
4. Children were given these when visiting the hospital for the dying
5. ____ New World
6. Recreational, stress-relieving drug
7. John's father
8. Director of Hatcheries and ____
9. He brought John The Complete Works of William Shakespeare
10. John compared Lenina to her
13. ____ Plus; highest caste
14. Bernard's last name
16. They do not need books to perform their social functions
18. Name of the deity in this world
19. Babies were conditioned to hate these and flowers

Brave New World

HELMHOLTZ	JULIET	PORGY	BRAVE	ODD
JOHN	TREATS	LENINA	HUXLEY	DEATH
DELTAS	BOOKS	FREE SPACE	IDENTICAL	LINDA
BOKANOVSKY	MITSIMA	MALPAIS	SOCIAL	POPE
MOTHER	COMMUNITY	DESTINY	CONDITIONING	MARX

Brave New World

RESERVATION	FORD	SOMA	HATCHERIES	HANGS
DIRECTOR	ISLAND	BOTTLE	CLAIM	SOLIDARITY
ALPHA	FEELIES	FREE SPACE	CONDITIONING	DESTINY
COMMUNITY	MOTHER	POPE	SOCIAL	MALPAIS
MITSIMA	BOKANOVSKY	LINDA	IDENTICAL	NINE

Brave New World

MITSIMA	RESERVATION	TREATS	DESTINY	FORD
JOHN	BRAVE	BOTTLE	PORGY	HANGS
CLAIM	SOCIAL	FREE SPACE	JULIET	LINDA
IDENTICAL	DEATH	SOLIDARITY	CONDITIONING	COMMUNITY
NINE	ODD	ALPHA	HATCHERIES	HUXLEY

Brave New World

DIRECTOR	BOOKS	MALPAIS	POPE	LENINA
FEELIES	MOTHER	MARX	BOKANOVSKY	HELMHOLTZ
SOMA	ISLAND	FREE SPACE	HATCHERIES	ALPHA
ODD	NINE	COMMUNITY	CONDITIONING	SOLIDARITY
DEATH	IDENTICAL	LINDA	JULIET	DELTAS

Brave New World

SOCIAL	DESTINY	JOHN	CLAIM	BOOKS
ODD	BRAVE	HUXLEY	POPE	MITSIMA
ALPHA	BOTTLE	FREE SPACE	DEATH	SOLIDARITY
DIRECTOR	LINDA	IDENTICAL	TREATS	PORGY
HATCHERIES	MALPAIS	BOKANOVSKY	FORD	MOTHER

Brave New World

LENINA	HELMHOLTZ	HANGS	COMMUNITY	SOMA
RESERVATION	CONDITIONING	NINE	JULIET	MARX
FEELIES	DELTAS	FREE SPACE	FORD	BOKANOVSKY
MALPAIS	HATCHERIES	PORGY	TREATS	IDENTICAL
LINDA	DIRECTOR	SOLIDARITY	DEATH	ISLAND

Brave New World

COMMUNITY	HELMHOLTZ	BOKANOVSKY	MARX	ISLAND
DELTAS	ODD	POPE	DEATH	DESTINY
NINE	MALPAIS	FREE SPACE	JULIET	SOCIAL
LINDA	JOHN	MOTHER	HUXLEY	FEELIES
PORGY	BRAVE	FORD	LENINA	HATCHERIES

Brave New World

BOTTLE	BOOKS	TREATS	CLAIM	ALPHA
SOMA	IDENTICAL	CONDITIONING	SOLIDARITY	RESERVATION
MITSIMA	DIRECTOR	FREE SPACE	LENINA	FORD
BRAVE	PORGY	FEELIES	HUXLEY	MOTHER
JOHN	LINDA	SOCIAL	JULIET	HANGS

Brave New World

ALPHA	HANGS	CONDITIONING	CLAIM	MITSIMA
DELTAS	MARX	MALPAIS	DIRECTOR	SOCIAL
RESERVATION	TREATS	FREE SPACE	JULIET	LINDA
SOLIDARITY	ODD	SOMA	BOTTLE	HATCHERIES
JOHN	FORD	ISLAND	MOTHER	BOKANOVSKY

Brave New World

BRAVE	POPE	FEELIES	COMMUNITY	BOOKS
LENINA	HUXLEY	DESTINY	HELMHOLTZ	NINE
DEATH	IDENTICAL	FREE SPACE	MOTHER	ISLAND
FORD	JOHN	HATCHERIES	BOTTLE	SOMA
ODD	SOLIDARITY	LINDA	JULIET	PORGY

Brave New World

NINE	FORD	JOHN	FEELIES	SOLIDARITY
BOKANOVSKY	ALPHA	MITSIMA	BRAVE	SOCIAL
HANGS	JULIET	FREE SPACE	HELMHOLTZ	CONDITIONING
SOMA	DELTAS	BOTTLE	MOTHER	TREATS
HATCHERIES	BOOKS	PORGY	MALPAIS	MARX

Brave New World

ISLAND	DIRECTOR	HUXLEY	DESTINY	CLAIM
LENINA	POPE	LINDA	ODD	IDENTICAL
DEATH	COMMUNITY	FREE SPACE	MALPAIS	PORGY
BOOKS	HATCHERIES	TREATS	MOTHER	BOTTLE
DELTAS	SOMA	CONDITIONING	HELMHOLTZ	RESERVATION

Brave New World

BOKANOVSKY	ALPHA	NINE	MALPAIS	CONDITIONING
BOOKS	SOLIDARITY	PORGY	FORD	BOTTLE
FEELIES	CLAIM	FREE SPACE	COMMUNITY	JOHN
ISLAND	TREATS	HUXLEY	HANGS	MITSIMA
DEATH	BRAVE	DIRECTOR	JULIET	SOCIAL

Brave New World

MARX	DELTAS	LENINA	MOTHER	DESTINY
SOMA	LINDA	RESERVATION	POPE	ODD
HATCHERIES	HELMHOLTZ	FREE SPACE	JULIET	DIRECTOR
BRAVE	DEATH	MITSIMA	HANGS	HUXLEY
TREATS	ISLAND	JOHN	COMMUNITY	IDENTICAL

Brave New World

PORGY	JULIET	LENINA	BOOKS	CONDITIONING
BOKANOVSKY	MALPAIS	HANGS	JOHN	NINE
ISLAND	FORD	FREE SPACE	BRAVE	MITSIMA
SOCIAL	HELMHOLTZ	RESERVATION	BOTTLE	DELTAS
IDENTICAL	MARX	ALPHA	POPE	CLAIM

Brave New World

DESTINY	COMMUNITY	HUXLEY	TREATS	SOMA
FEELIES	DEATH	SOLIDARITY	ODD	MOTHER
LINDA	HATCHERIES	FREE SPACE	POPE	ALPHA
MARX	IDENTICAL	DELTAS	BOTTLE	RESERVATION
HELMHOLTZ	SOCIAL	MITSIMA	BRAVE	DIRECTOR

Brave New World

MALPAIS	PORGY	IDENTICAL	NINE	ISLAND
HANGS	ALPHA	SOLIDARITY	RESERVATION	CLAIM
DESTINY	CONDITIONING	FREE SPACE	LINDA	LENINA
HATCHERIES	JULIET	HELMHOLTZ	HUXLEY	FORD
BOKANOVSKY	DIRECTOR	SOCIAL	POPE	TREATS

Brave New World

DELTAS	MARX	BOOKS	COMMUNITY	MOTHER
SOMA	FEELIES	ODD	JOHN	BRAVE
MITSIMA	DEATH	FREE SPACE	POPE	SOCIAL
DIRECTOR	BOKANOVSKY	FORD	HUXLEY	HELMHOLTZ
JULIET	HATCHERIES	LENINA	LINDA	BOTTLE

Brave New World

MALPAIS	DEATH	ODD	SOLIDARITY	HATCHERIES
BOKANOVSKY	HUXLEY	POPE	LINDA	BOTTLE
FORD	MOTHER	FREE SPACE	DIRECTOR	ISLAND
ALPHA	CONDITIONING	SOMA	DELTAS	TREATS
BOOKS	FEELIES	JULIET	JOHN	LENINA

Brave New World

BRAVE	MARX	MITSIMA	HELMHOLTZ	RESERVATION
DESTINY	COMMUNITY	CLAIM	SOCIAL	PORGY
NINE	HANGS	FREE SPACE	JOHN	JULIET
FEELIES	BOOKS	TREATS	DELTAS	SOMA
CONDITIONING	ALPHA	ISLAND	DIRECTOR	IDENTICAL

Brave New World

IDENTICAL	DELTAS	HATCHERIES	SOLIDARITY	LENINA
HUXLEY	NINE	DIRECTOR	FEELIES	CONDITIONING
BRAVE	DESTINY	FREE SPACE	BOTTLE	ODD
MITSIMA	HELMHOLTZ	RESERVATION	TREATS	SOCIAL
MOTHER	PORGY	DEATH	LINDA	ALPHA

Brave New World

SOMA	COMMUNITY	BOOKS	MARX	MALPAIS
ISLAND	JULIET	JOHN	HANGS	CLAIM
BOKANOVSKY	POPE	FREE SPACE	LINDA	DEATH
PORGY	MOTHER	SOCIAL	TREATS	RESERVATION
HELMHOLTZ	MITSIMA	ODD	BOTTLE	FORD

Brave New World

COMMUNITY	HANGS	POPE	MOTHER	SOCIAL
DELTAS	LINDA	TREATS	IDENTICAL	DIRECTOR
ODD	MALPAIS	FREE SPACE	SOLIDARITY	MARX
LENINA	FORD	SOMA	CONDITIONING	HELMHOLTZ
PORGY	JOHN	NINE	DESTINY	HATCHERIES

Brave New World

RESERVATION	CLAIM	HUXLEY	DEATH	FEELIES
ISLAND	BRAVE	BOTTLE	MITSIMA	BOOKS
JULIET	BOKANOVSKY	FREE SPACE	DESTINY	NINE
JOHN	PORGY	HELMHOLTZ	CONDITIONING	SOMA
FORD	LENINA	MARX	SOLIDARITY	ALPHA

Brave New World

IDENTICAL	BRAVE	RESERVATION	MALPAIS	DESTINY
BOKANOVSKY	NINE	DIRECTOR	HELMHOLTZ	FORD
FEELIES	HUXLEY	FREE SPACE	DELTAS	BOTTLE
HATCHERIES	ALPHA	MITSIMA	CLAIM	MARX
POPE	JOHN	COMMUNITY	HANGS	ISLAND

Brave New World

SOLIDARITY	SOCIAL	DEATH	BOOKS	JULIET
SOMA	LENINA	CONDITIONING	LINDA	PORGY
ODD	MOTHER	FREE SPACE	HANGS	COMMUNITY
JOHN	POPE	MARX	CLAIM	MITSIMA
ALPHA	HATCHERIES	BOTTLE	DELTAS	TREATS

Brave New World

ODD	BOTTLE	IDENTICAL	MARX	BOKANOVSKY
JULIET	BOOKS	HATCHERIES	LINDA	HUXLEY
DEATH	SOLIDARITY	FREE SPACE	ISLAND	JOHN
CONDITIONING	BRAVE	HANGS	POPE	SOMA
TREATS	PORGY	MOTHER	HELMHOLTZ	MITSIMA

Brave New World

SOCIAL	FORD	ALPHA	RESERVATION	DIRECTOR
NINE	MALPAIS	FEELIES	DELTAS	CLAIM
LENINA	COMMUNITY	FREE SPACE	HELMHOLTZ	MOTHER
PORGY	TREATS	SOMA	POPE	HANGS
BRAVE	CONDITIONING	JOHN	ISLAND	DESTINY

Brave New World

MOTHER	SOCIAL	SOMA	ODD	DEATH
HUXLEY	ISLAND	CLAIM	HELMHOLTZ	PORGY
FEELIES	TREATS	FREE SPACE	ALPHA	MARX
MITSIMA	HATCHERIES	BOTTLE	HANGS	BOKANOVSKY
FORD	DELTAS	DIRECTOR	LENINA	BOOKS

Brave New World

IDENTICAL	RESERVATION	LINDA	JULIET	JOHN
CONDITIONING	SOLIDARITY	BRAVE	NINE	DESTINY
COMMUNITY	MALPAIS	FREE SPACE	LENINA	DIRECTOR
DELTAS	FORD	BOKANOVSKY	HANGS	BOTTLE
HATCHERIES	MITSIMA	MARX	ALPHA	POPE

Brave New World

SOLIDARITY	TREATS	BOTTLE	ISLAND	JULIET
CLAIM	ALPHA	DIRECTOR	NINE	CONDITIONING
MARX	MITSIMA	FREE SPACE	HANGS	FORD
ODD	HELMHOLTZ	FEELIES	DEATH	LINDA
HATCHERIES	MOTHER	SOCIAL	JOHN	LENINA

Brave New World

IDENTICAL	BRAVE	HUXLEY	COMMUNITY	BOKANOVSKY
POPE	DELTAS	MALPAIS	RESERVATION	DESTINY
BOOKS	SOMA	FREE SPACE	JOHN	SOCIAL
MOTHER	HATCHERIES	LINDA	DEATH	FEELIES
HELMHOLTZ	ODD	FORD	HANGS	PORGY

Brave New World Vocabulary Word List

No.	Word	Clue/Definition
1.	ANNIHILATING	Completely overwhelming or incapacitating
2.	APPALLING	Shocking
3.	APPREHENSIVELY	Anxiously
4.	ASSET	Thing of value
5.	AXIOMATIC	Self-evident; not needing proof
6.	BENEVOLENTLY	Harmlessly; in a beneficial way
7.	BESTIAL	Lacking reason and intellect
8.	CAJOLERY	Urging with gentle and repeated appeals, teasing or flattery
9.	CARAPACE	Hard outer covering
10.	CASTE	Social class
11.	CHRONIC	Continual; recurring
12.	COMPUNCTION	Regret; remorse
13.	CONTEMPTUOUS	Disgraceful; disdainful; scornful
14.	DECONDITION	Become unconditioned; revert back to old ways
15.	ENDORSE	Give approval of or support to
16.	FLACCID	Flabby; listless
17.	FLAGRANTLY	Obviously; conspicuously
18.	GESTICULATING	Bodily movements, particularly for communication of an idea or for emphasis
19.	IGNOMINY	Disgrace
20.	IMPERCEPTIBLY	Unable to be detected by the senses
21.	IMPUNITY	Exemption from punishment
22.	INCONCEIVABLE	Unbelievable
23.	INDEFATIGABLY	Tirelessly
24.	INDULGENTLY	As if doing one a favor
25.	INEXORABLY	Relentlessly; without stopping
26.	INGRATIATING	Making oneself favorable to another
27.	INSURMOUNTABLE	Impossible to overcome
28.	INTRINSICALLY	Inherently; as a part of the nature of a thing itself
29.	IRRESOLUTE	Undecided
30.	LECHEROUS	Indulging in excessive sexual activity
31.	LUMINOUS	Enlightened; emitting light
32.	MONOGAMY	Practice of being married to one person at a time
33.	MORIBUND	About to die
34.	ODIOUS	Arousing a strong dislike or disgust
35.	OPTIMUM	Most favorable point
36.	ORDURE	Bodily waste; excrement
37.	PARENTHETICALLY	As if in parentheses; aside
38.	PATRONIZINGLY	In a condescending manner
39.	PLAINTIVE	Mournful
40.	PNEUMATIC	Filled with air
41.	POSTULATES	Rules or ideas that are taken for granted
42.	PRECIPICE	Cliff
43.	PRODIGIOUS	Impressively great
44.	PROLIFERATE	Multiply rapidly
45.	RECIPROCATED	Returned; mutually shared
46.	REPARATION	Compensation; something to make amends
47.	RUMINATING	Meditating; thinking
48.	SUBLIME	Noble; majestic; impressive
49.	SUBVERSIVE	Undermining; damaging to the authorities
50.	UNABASHED	Not disconcerted or embarrassed; calm

Brave New World Vocabulary Word List

No. Word	Clue/Definition
51. UNPRECEDENTED	Having never happened before
52. VITRIFIED	Made to look like glass

Brave New World Vocabulary Fill In The Blanks 1

1. Regret; remorse
2. Relentlessly; without stopping
3. Continual; recurring
4. Arousing a strong dislike or disgust
5. Not disconcerted or embarrassed; calm
6. Become unconditioned; revert back to old ways
7. Multiply rapidly
8. As if doing one a favor
9. Exemption from punishment
10. Shocking
11. Returned; mutually shared
12. About to die
13. Disgraceful; disdainful; scornful
14. Indulging in excessive sexual activity
15. Thing of value
16. Bodily movements, particularly for communication of an idea or for emphasis
17. Impressively great
18. Social class
19. Made to look like glass
20. Rules or ideas that are taken for granted

Brave New World Vocabulary Fill In The Blanks 1 Answer Key

COMPUNCTION	1. Regret; remorse
INEXORABLY	2. Relentlessly; without stopping
CHRONIC	3. Continual; recurring
ODIOUS	4. Arousing a strong dislike or disgust
UNABASHED	5. Not disconcerted or embarrassed; calm
DECONDITION	6. Become unconditioned; revert back to old ways
PROLIFERATE	7. Multiply rapidly
INDULGENTLY	8. As if doing one a favor
IMPUNITY	9. Exemption from punishment
APPALLING	10. Shocking
RECIPROCATED	11. Returned; mutually shared
MORIBUND	12. About to die
CONTEMPTUOUS	13. Disgraceful; disdainful; scornful
LECHEROUS	14. Indulging in excessive sexual activity
ASSET	15. Thing of value
GESTICULATING	16. Bodily movements, particularly for communication of an idea or for emphasis
PRODIGIOUS	17. Impressively great
CASTE	18. Social class
VITRIFIED	19. Made to look like glass
POSTULATES	20. Rules or ideas that are taken for granted

Brave New World Vocabulary Fill In The Blanks 2

_____   1. Completely overwhelming or incapacitating

_____   2. Meditating; thinking

_____   3. Exemption from punishment

_____   4. Urging with gentle and repeated appeals, teasing or flattery

_____   5. Obviously; conspicuously

_____   6. Bodily movements, particularly for communication of an idea or for emphasis

_____   7. Thing of value

_____   8. Filled with air

_____   9. Practice of being married to one person at a time

_____   10. Anxiously

_____   11. Self-evident; not needing proof

_____   12. Returned; mutually shared

_____   13. Impossible to overcome

_____   14. Multiply rapidly

_____   15. Regret; remorse

_____   16. Making oneself favorable to another

_____   17. As if in parentheses; aside

_____   18. Having never happened before

_____   19. Undermining; damaging to the authorities

_____   20. Enlightened; emitting light

Brave New World Vocabulary Fill In The Blanks 2 Answer Key

ANNIHILATING	1. Completely overwhelming or incapacitating
RUMINATING	2. Meditating; thinking
IMPUNITY	3. Exemption from punishment
CAJOLERY	4. Urging with gentle and repeated appeals, teasing or flattery
FLAGRANTLY	5. Obviously; conspicuously
GESTICULATING	6. Bodily movements, particularly for communication of an idea or for emphasis
ASSET	7. Thing of value
PNEUMATIC	8. Filled with air
MONOGAMY	9. Practice of being married to one person at a time
APPREHENSIVELY	10. Anxiously
AXIOMATIC	11. Self-evident; not needing proof
RECIPROCATED	12. Returned; mutually shared
INSURMOUNTABLE	13. Impossible to overcome
PROLIFERATE	14. Multiply rapidly
COMPUNCTION	15. Regret; remorse
INGRATIATING	16. Making oneself favorable to another
PARENTHETICALLY	17. As if in parentheses; aside
UNPRECEDENTED	18. Having never happened before
SUBVERSIVE	19. Undermining; damaging to the authorities
LUMINOUS	20. Enlightened; emitting light

Brave New World Vocabulary Fill In The Blanks 3

1. Unbelievable
2. Bodily movements, particularly for communication of an idea or for emphasis
3. Made to look like glass
4. Not disconcerted or embarrassed; calm
5. Relentlessly; without stopping
6. As if doing one a favor
7. Rules or ideas that are taken for granted
8. Social class
9. Completely overwhelming or incapacitating
10. Give approval of or support to
11. Inherently; as a part of the nature of a thing itself
12. Filled with air
13. Undecided
14. Regret; remorse
15. Self-evident; not needing proof
16. Disgraceful; disdainful; scornful
17. Bodily waste; excrement
18. As if in parentheses; aside
19. Impressively great
20. Flabby; listless

Brave New World Vocabulary Fill In The Blanks 3 Answer Key

INCONCEIVABLE	1. Unbelievable
GESTICULATING	2. Bodily movements, particularly for communication of an idea or for emphasis
VITRIFIED	3. Made to look like glass
UNABASHED	4. Not disconcerted or embarrassed; calm
INEXORABLY	5. Relentlessly; without stopping
INDULGENTLY	6. As if doing one a favor
POSTULATES	7. Rules or ideas that are taken for granted
CASTE	8. Social class
ANNIHILATING	9. Completely overwhelming or incapacitating
ENDORSE	10. Give approval of or support to
INTRINSICALLY	11. Inherently; as a part of the nature of a thing itself
PNEUMATIC	12. Filled with air
IRRESOLUTE	13. Undecided
COMPUNCTION	14. Regret; remorse
AXIOMATIC	15. Self-evident; not needing proof
CONTEMPTUOUS	16. Disgraceful; disdainful; scornful
ORDURE	17. Bodily waste; excrement
PARENTHETICALLY	18. As if in parentheses; aside
PRODIGIOUS	19. Impressively great
FLACCID	20. Flabby; listless

Brave New World Vocabulary Fill In The Blanks 4

_____   1. Impossible to overcome

_____   2. Most favorable point

_____   3. Lacking reason and intellect

_____   4. Rules or ideas that are taken for granted

_____   5. Compensation; something to make amends

_____   6. As if in parentheses; aside

_____   7. Social class

_____   8. Arousing a strong dislike or disgust

_____   9. Meditating; thinking

_____   10. Anxiously

_____   11. Disgraceful; disdainful; scornful

_____   12. Indulging in excessive sexual activity

_____   13. Undecided

_____   14. Completely overwhelming or incapacitating

_____   15. As if doing one a favor

_____   16. Making oneself favorable to another

_____   17. Practice of being married to one person at a time

_____   18. Tirelessly

_____   19. Disgrace

_____   20. Filled with air

Brave New World Vocabulary Fill In The Blanks 4 Answer Key

INSURMOUNTABLE	1. Impossible to overcome
OPTIMUM	2. Most favorable point
BESTIAL	3. Lacking reason and intellect
POSTULATES	4. Rules or ideas that are taken for granted
REPARATION	5. Compensation; something to make amends
PARENTHETICALLY	6. As if in parentheses; aside
CASTE	7. Social class
ODIOUS	8. Arousing a strong dislike or disgust
RUMINATING	9. Meditating; thinking
APPREHENSIVELY	10. Anxiously
CONTEMPTUOUS	11. Disgraceful; disdainful; scornful
LECHEROUS	12. Indulging in excessive sexual activity
IRRESOLUTE	13. Undecided
ANNIHILATING	14. Completely overwhelming or incapacitating
INDULGENTLY	15. As if doing one a favor
INGRATIATING	16. Making oneself favorable to another
MONOGAMY	17. Practice of being married to one person at a time
INDEFATIGABLY	18. Tirelessly
IGNOMINY	19. Disgrace
PNEUMATIC	20. Filled with air

Brave New World Vocabulary Matching 1

___ 1. DECONDITION
___ 2. IMPERCEPTIBLY
___ 3. PRODIGIOUS
___ 4. PRECIPICE
___ 5. FLACCID
___ 6. SUBLIME
___ 7. IRRESOLUTE
___ 8. MORIBUND
___ 9. BENEVOLENTLY
___ 10. FLAGRANTLY
___ 11. INCONCEIVABLE
___ 12. UNPRECEDENTED
___ 13. PROLIFERATE
___ 14. RUMINATING
___ 15. ENDORSE
___ 16. ODIOUS
___ 17. BESTIAL
___ 18. INGRATIATING
___ 19. LECHEROUS
___ 20. ASSET
___ 21. IGNOMINY
___ 22. INSURMOUNTABLE
___ 23. APPREHENSIVELY
___ 24. CAJOLERY
___ 25. CARAPACE

A. Meditating; thinking
B. Urging with gentle and repeated appeals, teasing or flattery
C. Multiply rapidly
D. Making oneself favorable to another
E. Unable to be detected by the senses
F. Having never happened before
G. Hard outer covering
H. About to die
I. Flabby; listless
J. Give approval of or support to
K. Anxiously
L. Noble; majestic; impressive
M. Cliff
N. Disgrace
O. Lacking reason and intellect
P. Thing of value
Q. Indulging in excessive sexual activity
R. Undecided
S. Harmlessly; in a beneficial way
T. Unbelievable
U. Obviously; conspicuously
V. Impossible to overcome
W. Arousing a strong dislike or disgust
X. Become unconditioned; revert back to old ways
Y. Impressively great

Brave New World Vocabulary Matching 1 Answer Key

X - 1. DECONDITION	A.	Meditating; thinking
E - 2. IMPERCEPTIBLY	B.	Urging with gentle and repeated appeals, teasing or flattery
Y - 3. PRODIGIOUS	C.	Multiply rapidly
M - 4. PRECIPICE	D.	Making oneself favorable to another
I - 5. FLACCID	E.	Unable to be detected by the senses
L - 6. SUBLIME	F.	Having never happened before
R - 7. IRRESOLUTE	G.	Hard outer covering
H - 8. MORIBUND	H.	About to die
S - 9. BENEVOLENTLY	I.	Flabby; listless
U - 10. FLAGRANTLY	J.	Give approval of or support to
T - 11. INCONCEIVABLE	K.	Anxiously
F - 12. UNPRECEDENTED	L.	Noble; majestic; impressive
C - 13. PROLIFERATE	M.	Cliff
A - 14. RUMINATING	N.	Disgrace
J - 15. ENDORSE	O.	Lacking reason and intellect
W - 16. ODIOUS	P.	Thing of value
O - 17. BESTIAL	Q.	Indulging in excessive sexual activity
D - 18. INGRATIATING	R.	Undecided
Q - 19. LECHEROUS	S.	Harmlessly; in a beneficial way
P - 20. ASSET	T.	Unbelievable
N - 21. IGNOMINY	U.	Obviously; conspicuously
V - 22. INSURMOUNTABLE	V.	Impossible to overcome
K - 23. APPREHENSIVELY	W.	Arousing a strong dislike or disgust
B - 24. CAJOLERY	X.	Become unconditioned; revert back to old ways
G - 25. CARAPACE	Y.	Impressively great

Brave New World Vocabulary Matching 2

___ 1. LUMINOUS   A. Made to look like glass
___ 2. INDULGENTLY   B. Undecided
___ 3. POSTULATES   C. Disgrace
___ 4. PNEUMATIC   D. Unable to be detected by the senses
___ 5. AXIOMATIC   E. Continual; recurring
___ 6. VITRIFIED   F. Tirelessly
___ 7. IMPERCEPTIBLY   G. Harmlessly; in a beneficial way
___ 8. CARAPACE   H. Having never happened before
___ 9. CASTE   I. Hard outer covering
___10. REPARATION   J. Self-evident; not needing proof
___11. PATRONIZINGLY   K. Rules or ideas that are taken for granted
___12. INEXORABLY   L. Exemption from punishment
___13. IMPUNITY   M. As if doing one a favor
___14. IGNOMINY   N. In a condescending manner
___15. INCONCEIVABLE   O. Become unconditioned; revert back to old ways
___16. SUBVERSIVE   P. Unbelievable
___17. FLAGRANTLY   Q. Enlightened; emitting light
___18. CHRONIC   R. Filled with air
___19. INDEFATIGABLY   S. Compensation; something to make amends
___20. INSURMOUNTABLE T. Anxiously
___21. UNPRECEDENTED   U. Relentlessly; without stopping
___22. BENEVOLENTLY   V. Impossible to overcome
___23. APPREHENSIVELY W. Obviously; conspicuously
___24. DECONDITION   X. Undermining; damaging to the authorities
___25. IRRESOLUTE   Y. Social class

Brave New World Vocabulary Matching 2 Answer Key

Q - 1. LUMINOUS		A. Made to look like glass
M - 2. INDULGENTLY		B. Undecided
K - 3. POSTULATES		C. Disgrace
R - 4. PNEUMATIC		D. Unable to be detected by the senses
J - 5. AXIOMATIC		E. Continual; recurring
A - 6. VITRIFIED		F. Tirelessly
D - 7. IMPERCEPTIBLY		G. Harmlessly; in a beneficial way
I - 8. CARAPACE		H. Having never happened before
Y - 9. CASTE		I. Hard outer covering
S - 10. REPARATION		J. Self-evident; not needing proof
N - 11. PATRONIZINGLY		K. Rules or ideas that are taken for granted
U - 12. INEXORABLY		L. Exemption from punishment
L - 13. IMPUNITY		M. As if doing one a favor
C - 14. IGNOMINY		N. In a condescending manner
P - 15. INCONCEIVABLE		O. Become unconditioned; revert back to old ways
X - 16. SUBVERSIVE		P. Unbelievable
W - 17. FLAGRANTLY		Q. Enlightened; emitting light
E - 18. CHRONIC		R. Filled with air
F - 19. INDEFATIGABLY		S. Compensation; something to make amends
V - 20. INSURMOUNTABLE		T. Anxiously
H - 21. UNPRECEDENTED		U. Relentlessly; without stopping
G - 22. BENEVOLENTLY		V. Impossible to overcome
T - 23. APPREHENSIVELY		W. Obviously; conspicuously
O - 24. DECONDITION		X. Undermining; damaging to the authorities
B - 25. IRRESOLUTE		Y. Social class

Brave New World Vocabulary Matching 3

___ 1. ENDORSE
___ 2. ASSET
___ 3. VITRIFIED
___ 4. MONOGAMY
___ 5. MORIBUND
___ 6. GESTICULATING
___ 7. LECHEROUS
___ 8. PARENTHETICALLY
___ 9. COMPUNCTION
___10. REPARATION
___11. FLAGRANTLY
___12. OPTIMUM
___13. DECONDITION
___14. CARAPACE
___15. IMPERCEPTIBLY
___16. AXIOMATIC
___17. POSTULATES
___18. PLAINTIVE
___19. IRRESOLUTE
___20. BENEVOLENTLY
___21. INDEFATIGABLY
___22. PNEUMATIC
___23. RECIPROCATED
___24. INDULGENTLY
___25. SUBVERSIVE

A. Rules or ideas that are taken for granted
B. Tirelessly
C. As if in parentheses; aside
D. Become unconditioned; revert back to old ways
E. Practice of being married to one person at a time
F. About to die
G. Undermining; damaging to the authorities
H. Most favorable point
I. Regret; remorse
J. As if doing one a favor
K. Hard outer covering
L. Obviously; conspicuously
M. Bodily movements, particularly for communication of an idea or for emphasis
N. Filled with air
O. Compensation; something to make amends
P. Self-evident; not needing proof
Q. Made to look like glass
R. Unable to be detected by the senses
S. Indulging in excessive sexual activity
T. Give approval of or support to
U. Returned; mutually shared
V. Mournful
W. Thing of value
X. Undecided
Y. Harmlessly; in a beneficial way

Brave New World Vocabulary Matching 3 Answer Key

T - 1. ENDORSE	A.	Rules or ideas that are taken for granted
W - 2. ASSET	B.	Tirelessly
Q - 3. VITRIFIED	C.	As if in parentheses; aside
E - 4. MONOGAMY	D.	Become unconditioned; revert back to old ways
F - 5. MORIBUND	E.	Practice of being married to one person at a time
M - 6. GESTICULATING	F.	About to die
S - 7. LECHEROUS	G.	Undermining; damaging to the authorities
C - 8. PARENTHETICALLY	H.	Most favorable point
I - 9. COMPUNCTION	I.	Regret; remorse
O - 10. REPARATION	J.	As if doing one a favor
L - 11. FLAGRANTLY	K.	Hard outer covering
H - 12. OPTIMUM	L.	Obviously; conspicuously
D - 13. DECONDITION	M.	Bodily movements, particularly for communication of an idea or for emphasis
K - 14. CARAPACE	N.	Filled with air
R - 15. IMPERCEPTIBLY	O.	Compensation; something to make amends
P - 16. AXIOMATIC	P.	Self-evident; not needing proof
A - 17. POSTULATES	Q.	Made to look like glass
V - 18. PLAINTIVE	R.	Unable to be detected by the senses
X - 19. IRRESOLUTE	S.	Indulging in excessive sexual activity
Y - 20. BENEVOLENTLY	T.	Give approval of or support to
B - 21. INDEFATIGABLY	U.	Returned; mutually shared
N - 22. PNEUMATIC	V.	Mournful
U - 23. RECIPROCATED	W.	Thing of value
J - 24. INDULGENTLY	X.	Undecided
G - 25. SUBVERSIVE	Y.	Harmlessly; in a beneficial way

Brave New World Vocabulary Matching 4

___ 1. PATRONIZINGLY A. Hard outer covering
___ 2. IGNOMINY B. Urging with gentle and repeated appeals, teasing or flattery
___ 3. SUBVERSIVE C. Filled with air
___ 4. BENEVOLENTLY D. Arousing a strong dislike or disgust
___ 5. RECIPROCATED E. Lacking reason and intellect
___ 6. UNPRECEDENTED F. Undermining; damaging to the authorities
___ 7. INSURMOUNTABLE G. Not disconcerted or embarrassed; calm
___ 8. FLAGRANTLY H. Disgrace
___ 9. BESTIAL I. Regret; remorse
___10. CHRONIC J. Multiply rapidly
___11. UNABASHED K. Relentlessly; without stopping
___12. MORIBUND L. Completely overwhelming or incapacitating
___13. INEXORABLY M. Continual; recurring
___14. ANNIHILATING N. Meditating; thinking
___15. COMPUNCTION O. About to die
___16. CARAPACE P. Returned; mutually shared
___17. PROLIFERATE Q. Indulging in excessive sexual activity
___18. RUMINATING R. Impossible to overcome
___19. LECHEROUS S. Disgraceful; disdainful; scornful
___20. OPTIMUM T. Obviously; conspicuously
___21. CONTEMPTUOUS U. Enlightened; emitting light
___22. ODIOUS V. Having never happened before
___23. PNEUMATIC W. Most favorable point
___24. CAJOLERY X. Harmlessly; in a beneficial way
___25. LUMINOUS Y. In a condescending manner

Brave New World Vocabulary Matching 4 Answer Key

Y - 1. PATRONIZINGLY	A. Hard outer covering
H - 2. IGNOMINY	B. Urging with gentle and repeated appeals, teasing or flattery
F - 3. SUBVERSIVE	C. Filled with air
X - 4. BENEVOLENTLY	D. Arousing a strong dislike or disgust
P - 5. RECIPROCATED	E. Lacking reason and intellect
V - 6. UNPRECEDENTED	F. Undermining; damaging to the authorities
R - 7. INSURMOUNTABLE	G. Not disconcerted or embarrassed; calm
T - 8. FLAGRANTLY	H. Disgrace
E - 9. BESTIAL	I. Regret; remorse
M - 10. CHRONIC	J. Multiply rapidly
G - 11. UNABASHED	K. Relentlessly; without stopping
O - 12. MORIBUND	L. Completely overwhelming or incapacitating
K - 13. INEXORABLY	M. Continual; recurring
L - 14. ANNIHILATING	N. Meditating; thinking
I - 15. COMPUNCTION	O. About to die
A - 16. CARAPACE	P. Returned; mutually shared
J - 17. PROLIFERATE	Q. Indulging in excessive sexual activity
N - 18. RUMINATING	R. Impossible to overcome
Q - 19. LECHEROUS	S. Disgraceful; disdainful; scornful
W - 20. OPTIMUM	T. Obviously; conspicuously
S - 21. CONTEMPTUOUS	U. Enlightened; emitting light
D - 22. ODIOUS	V. Having never happened before
C - 23. PNEUMATIC	W. Most favorable point
B - 24. CAJOLERY	X. Harmlessly; in a beneficial way
U - 25. LUMINOUS	Y. In a condescending manner

Brave New World Vocabulary Magic Squares 1

Match the definition with the vocabulary word. Put your answers in the magic squares below. When your answers are correct, all columns and rows will add to the same number.

A. DECONDITION
B. IMPUNITY
C. SUBVERSIVE
D. SUBLIME
E. IRRESOLUTE
F. CONTEMPTUOUS
G. CASTE
H. ODIOUS
I. APPREHENSIVELY
J. CAJOLERY
K. VITRIFIED
L. UNPRECEDENTED
M. INEXORABLY
N. INDULGENTLY
O. INDEFATIGABLY
P. FLACCID

1. Tirelessly
2. Noble; majestic; impressive
3. Urging with gentle and repeated appeals, teasing or flattery
4. Undecided
5. Anxiously
6. Disgraceful; disdainful; scornful
7. Flabby; listless
8. Undermining; damaging to the authorities
9. Arousing a strong dislike or disgust
10. Made to look like glass
11. Become unconditioned; revert back to old ways
12. As if doing one a favor
13. Exemption from punishment
14. Relentlessly; without stopping
15. Social class
16. Having never happened before

A=	B=	C=	D=
E=	F=	G=	H=
I=	J=	K=	L=
M=	N=	O=	P=

Brave New World Vocabulary Magic Squares 1 Answer Key

Match the definition with the vocabulary word. Put your answers in the magic squares below. When your answers are correct, all columns and rows will add to the same number.

A. DECONDITION
B. IMPUNITY
C. SUBVERSIVE
D. SUBLIME
E. IRRESOLUTE
F. CONTEMPTUOUS
G. CASTE
H. ODIOUS
I. APPREHENSIVELY
J. CAJOLERY
K. VITRIFIED
L. UNPRECEDENTED
M. INEXORABLY
N. INDULGENTLY
O. INDEFATIGABLY
P. FLACCID

1. Tirelessly
2. Noble; majestic; impressive
3. Urging with gentle and repeated appeals, teasing or flattery
4. Undecided
5. Anxiously
6. Disgraceful; disdainful; scornful
7. Flabby; listless
8. Undermining; damaging to the authorities
9. Arousing a strong dislike or disgust
10. Made to look like glass
11. Become unconditioned; revert back to old ways
12. As if doing one a favor
13. Exemption from punishment
14. Relentlessly; without stopping
15. Social class
16. Having never happened before

A=11	B=13	C=8	D=2
E=4	F=6	G=15	H=9
I=5	J=3	K=10	L=16
M=14	N=12	O=1	P=7

Copyrighted

Brave New World Vocabulary Magic Squares 2

Match the definition with the vocabulary word. Put your answers in the magic squares below. When your answers are correct, all columns and rows will add to the same number.

A. RECIPROCATED
B. AXIOMATIC
C. CARAPACE
D. IMPUNITY
E. BENEVOLENTLY
F. ODIOUS
G. LUMINOUS
H. PATRONIZINGLY
I. BESTIAL
J. ENDORSE
K. ORDURE
L. INDEFATIGABLY
M. MONOGAMY
N. RUMINATING
O. UNPRECEDENTED
P. FLAGRANTLY

1. Returned; mutually shared
2. Meditating; thinking
3. Give approval of or support to
4. Harmlessly; in a beneficial way
5. Enlightened; emitting light
6. Tirelessly
7. Obviously; conspicuously
8. Hard outer covering
9. Having never happened before
10. Exemption from punishment
11. In a condescending manner
12. Bodily waste; excrement
13. Lacking reason and intellect
14. Arousing a strong dislike or disgust
15. Self-evident; not needing proof
16. Practice of being married to one person at a time

A=	B=	C=	D=
E=	F=	G=	H=
I=	J=	K=	L=
M=	N=	O=	P=

Brave New World Vocabulary Magic Squares 2 Answer Key

Match the definition with the vocabulary word. Put your answers in the magic squares below. When your answers are correct, all columns and rows will add to the same number.

A. RECIPROCATED
B. AXIOMATIC
C. CARAPACE
D. IMPUNITY
E. BENEVOLENTLY
F. ODIOUS
G. LUMINOUS
H. PATRONIZINGLY
I. BESTIAL
J. ENDORSE
K. ORDURE
L. INDEFATIGABLY
M. MONOGAMY
N. RUMINATING
O. UNPRECEDENTED
P. FLAGRANTLY

1. Returned; mutually shared
2. Meditating; thinking
3. Give approval of or support to
4. Harmlessly; in a beneficial way
5. Enlightened; emitting light
6. Tirelessly
7. Obviously; conspicuously
8. Hard outer covering
9. Having never happened before
10. Exemption from punishment
11. In a condescending manner
12. Bodily waste; excrement
13. Lacking reason and intellect
14. Arousing a strong dislike or disgust
15. Self-evident; not needing proof
16. Practice of being married to one person at a time

A=1	B=15	C=8	D=10
E=4	F=14	G=5	H=11
I=13	J=3	K=12	L=6
M=16	N=2	O=9	P=7

Brave New World Vocabulary Magic Squares 3

Match the definition with the vocabulary word. Put your answers in the magic squares below. When your answers are correct, all columns and rows will add to the same number.

A. PROLIFERATE
B. INGRATIATING
C. IMPERCEPTIBLY
D. PRECIPICE
E. PRODIGIOUS
F. DECONDITION
G. UNABASHED
H. ODIOUS
I. ENDORSE
J. MORIBUND
K. VITRIFIED
L. ANNIHILATING
M. RUMINATING
N. CAJOLERY
O. FLACCID
P. PATRONIZINGLY

1. Unable to be detected by the senses
2. About to die
3. Become unconditioned; revert back to old ways
4. Flabby; listless
5. In a condescending manner
6. Impressively great
7. Give approval of or support to
8. Cliff
9. Meditating; thinking
10. Arousing a strong dislike or disgust
11. Completely overwhelming or incapacitating
12. Multiply rapidly
13. Making oneself favorable to another
14. Made to look like glass
15. Not disconcerted or embarrassed; calm
16. Urging with gentle and repeated appeals, teasing or flattery

A=	B=	C=	D=
E=	F=	G=	H=
I=	J=	K=	L=
M=	N=	O=	P=

Brave New World Vocabulary Magic Squares 3 Answer Key

Match the definition with the vocabulary word. Put your answers in the magic squares below. When your answers are correct, all columns and rows will add to the same number.

A. PROLIFERATE
B. INGRATIATING
C. IMPERCEPTIBLY
D. PRECIPICE
E. PRODIGIOUS
F. DECONDITION
G. UNABASHED
H. ODIOUS
I. ENDORSE
J. MORIBUND
K. VITRIFIED
L. ANNIHILATING
M. RUMINATING
N. CAJOLERY
O. FLACCID
P. PATRONIZINGLY

1. Unable to be detected by the senses
2. About to die
3. Become unconditioned; revert back to old ways
4. Flabby; listless
5. In a condescending manner
6. Impressively great
7. Give approval of or support to
8. Cliff
9. Meditating; thinking
10. Arousing a strong dislike or disgust
11. Completely overwhelming or incapacitating
12. Multiply rapidly
13. Making oneself favorable to another
14. Made to look like glass
15. Not disconcerted or embarrassed; calm
16. Urging with gentle and repeated appeals, teasing or flattery

A=12	B=13	C=1	D=8
E=6	F=3	G=15	H=10
I=7	J=2	K=14	L=11
M=9	N=16	O=4	P=5

Brave New World Vocabulary Magic Squares 4

Match the definition with the vocabulary word. Put your answers in the magic squares below. When your answers are correct, all columns and rows will add to the same number.

A. REPARATION
B. UNPRECEDENTED
C. MONOGAMY
D. CHRONIC
E. UNABASHED
F. LECHEROUS
G. CASTE
H. OPTIMUM
I. LUMINOUS
J. ORDURE
K. IGNOMINY
L. FLAGRANTLY
M. PRECIPICE
N. APPALLING
O. SUBVERSIVE
P. BENEVOLENTLY

1. Undermining; damaging to the authorities
2. Bodily waste; excrement
3. Most favorable point
4. Compensation; something to make amends
5. Continual; recurring
6. Not disconcerted or embarrassed; calm
7. Disgrace
8. Shocking
9. Indulging in excessive sexual activity
10. Practice of being married to one person at a time
11. Cliff
12. Obviously; conspicuously
13. Enlightened; emitting light
14. Harmlessly; in a beneficial way
15. Having never happened before
16. Social class

A=	B=	C=	D=
E=	F=	G=	H=
I=	J=	K=	L=
M=	N=	O=	P=

Brave New World Vocabulary Magic Squares 4 Answer Key

Match the definition with the vocabulary word. Put your answers in the magic squares below. When your answers are correct, all columns and rows will add to the same number.

A. REPARATION
B. UNPRECEDENTED
C. MONOGAMY
D. CHRONIC
E. UNABASHED
F. LECHEROUS
G. CASTE
H. OPTIMUM
I. LUMINOUS
J. ORDURE
K. IGNOMINY
L. FLAGRANTLY
M. PRECIPICE
N. APPALLING
O. SUBVERSIVE
P. BENEVOLENTLY

1. Undermining; damaging to the authorities
2. Bodily waste; excrement
3. Most favorable point
4. Compensation; something to make amends
5. Continual; recurring
6. Not disconcerted or embarrassed; calm
7. Disgrace
8. Shocking
9. Indulging in excessive sexual activity
10. Practice of being married to one person at a time
11. Cliff
12. Obviously; conspicuously
13. Enlightened; emitting light
14. Harmlessly; in a beneficial way
15. Having never happened before
16. Social class

A=4	B=15	C=10	D=5
E=6	F=9	G=16	H=3
I=13	J=2	K=7	L=12
M=11	N=8	O=1	P=14

Brave New World Vocabulary Word Search 1

Words are placed backwards, forward, diagonally, up and down. Clues listed below can help you find the words. Circle the hidden vocabulary words in the maze.

V	I	T	R	I	F	I	E	D	D	P	N	W	I	P	V	C	J	I	Q
Y	S	E	K	W	X	Y	R	J	X	R	K	R	N	L	S	O	C	M	P
C	X	C	Q	N	S	W	J	X	Y	E	F	N	E	A	V	M	D	P	D
I	K	A	T	O	F	F	P	S	R	C	R	O	X	I	R	P	G	U	J
T	O	P	T	I	M	U	M	S	G	I	G	I	O	N	U	N	N	N	X
A	W	A	D	T	O	I	Y	Z	N	P	M	T	R	T	M	N	I	I	S
M	L	R	N	A	N	R	S	B	I	I	X	I	A	I	C	T	T	T	J
U	K	A	U	R	O	R	G	C	T	C	D	D	B	V	N	T	A	Y	P
E	C	C	B	A	G	E	L	K	A	E	Y	N	L	E	A	I	I	Y	L
N	N	F	I	P	A	S	L	X	L	S	F	O	Y	S	T	O	T	L	J
P	F	D	R	E	M	O	Y	E	U	X	T	C	S	P	I	N	A	E	V
V	T	A	O	R	Y	L	L	A	C	I	T	E	H	T	N	E	R	A	P
F	F	P	M	R	X	U	B	P	I	H	T	D	C	L	G	U	G	X	D
B	L	P	L	S	S	T	A	O	T	T	O	E	P	N	D	L	N	I	M
E	A	A	M	S	T	E	G	S	S	D	E	V	R	W	R	L	Q	O	W
S	G	L	C	L	E	B	I	T	E	I	N	N	O	O	U	J	X	G	M
T	R	L	G	C	V	L	T	U	G	O	Q	D	M	U	V	Z	B	M	T
I	A	I	Z	T	I	M	A	L	P	U	I	I	S	Y	S	L	N	A	J
A	N	N	W	T	S	D	F	A	F	S	N	G	B	U	J	X	C	T	G
L	T	G	Z	F	R	T	E	T	K	O	G	I	N	B	B	I	R	I	X
T	L	P	L	Y	E	Y	D	E	U	W	K	O	L	O	N	L	Y	C	G
V	Y	S	D	W	V	J	N	S	X	R	W	U	S	O	M	X	I	J	J
H	W	J	Q	K	B	M	I	H	W	N	Z	S	R	N	K	I	P	B	M
Q	F	R	D	W	U	W	D	V	Y	R	D	H	P	J	X	H	N	M	E
U	N	A	B	A	S	H	E	D	N	T	C	A	J	O	L	E	R	D	C
																		Y	

About to die (8)
Arousing a strong dislike or disgust (6)
As if in parentheses; aside (15)
Become unconditioned; revert back to old ways (11)
Bodily movements, particularly for communication of an idea or for emphasis (13)
Bodily waste; excrement (6)
Cliff (9)
Compensation; something to make amends (10)
Continual; recurring (7)
Disgrace (8)
Enlightened; emitting light (8)
Exemption from punishment (8)
Filled with air (9)
Flabby; listless (7)
Give approval of or support to (7)
Hard outer covering (8)
Impressively great (10)
Indulging in excessive sexual activity (9)
Lacking reason and intellect (7)

Made to look like glass (9)
Making oneself favorable to another (12)
Meditating; thinking (10)
Most favorable point (8)
Mournful (9)
Noble; majestic; impressive (7)
Not disconcerted or embarrassed; calm (9)
Obviously; conspicuously (10)
Practice of being married to one person at a time (8)
Regret; remorse (11)
Relentlessly; without stopping (10)
Rules or ideas that are taken for granted (10)
Self-evident; not needing proof (9)
Shocking (9)
Social class (5)
Thing of value (5)
Tirelessly (13)
Undecided (10)
Undermining; damaging to the authorities (10)
Urging with gentle and repeated appeals, teasing or flattery (8)

Brave New World Vocabulary Word Search 1 Answer Key

Words are placed backwards, forward, diagonally, up and down. Clues listed below can help you find the words. Circle the hidden vocabulary words in the maze.

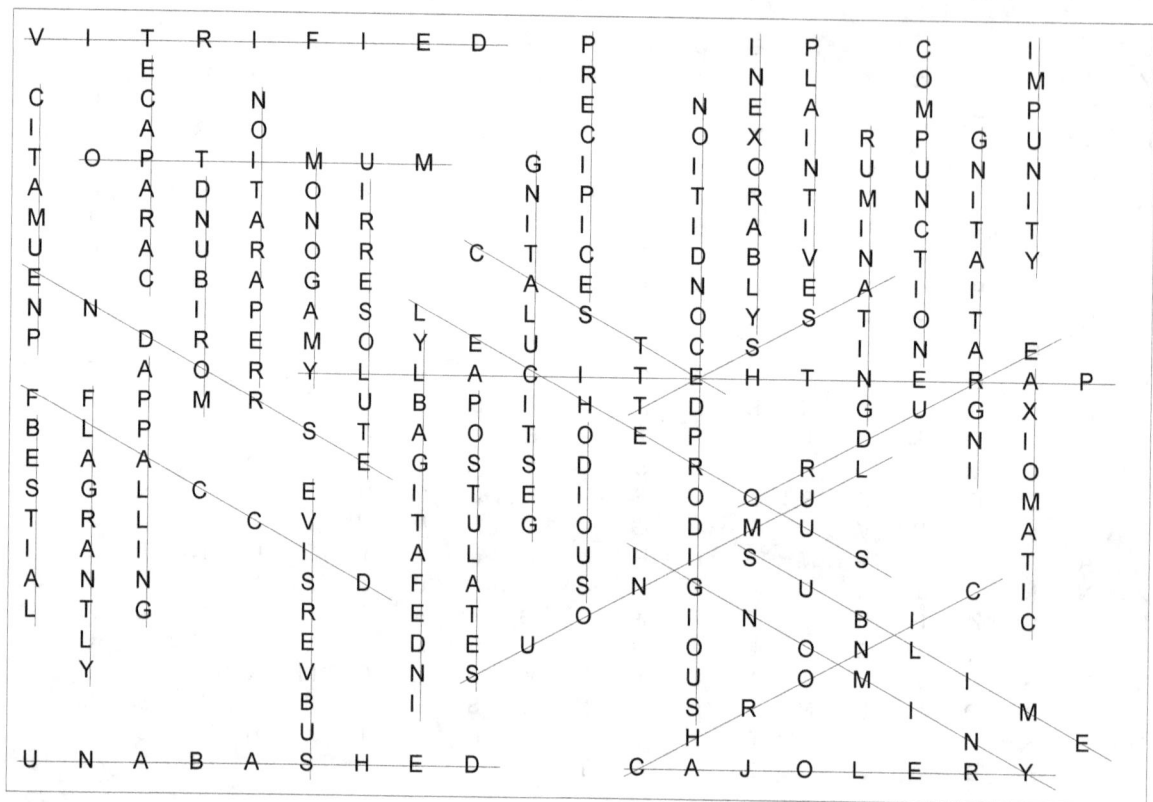

About to die (8)
Arousing a strong dislike or disgust (6)
As if in parentheses; aside (15)
Become unconditioned; revert back to old ways (11)
Bodily movements, particularly for communication of an idea or for emphasis (13)
Bodily waste; excrement (6)
Cliff (9)
Compensation; something to make amends (10)
Continual; recurring (7)
Disgrace (8)
Enlightened; emitting light (8)
Exemption from punishment (8)
Filled with air (9)
Flabby; listless (7)
Give approval of or support to (7)
Hard outer covering (8)
Impressively great (10)
Indulging in excessive sexual activity (9)
Lacking reason and intellect (7)

Made to look like glass (9)
Making oneself favorable to another (12)
Meditating; thinking (10)
Most favorable point (8)
Mournful (9)
Noble; majestic; impressive (7)
Not disconcerted or embarrassed; calm (9)
Obviously; conspicuously (10)
Practice of being married to one person at a time (8)
Regret; remorse (11)
Relentlessly; without stopping (10)
Rules or ideas that are taken for granted (10)
Self-evident; not needing proof (9)
Shocking (9)
Social class (5)
Thing of value (5)
Tirelessly (13)
Undecided (10)
Undermining; damaging to the authorities (10)
Urging with gentle and repeated appeals, teasing or flattery (8)

88
Copyrighted

Brave New World Vocabulary Word Search 2

Words are placed backwards, forward, diagonally, up and down. Clues listed below can help you find the words. Circle the hidden vocabulary words in the maze.

```
C D E C O N D I T I O N T M J X C A I N
O I K Y M A G O N O M N C Z M G A X N V
M R S Y J A J W R D Y X Q X L G R I T N
P R U R H P L E C H E R O U S W A O R C
U E O T B P E T A R E F I L O R P M I L
N S U R R R O V K P B P A Z V C A A N N
C O T P P R E S P F W L Q G T K L C T S P
T L P P R H R V T P B A F V I V E I I P
I U M N T E B C R I S Q I L X G F C C K
O T E O P N C O Y D M P S N A Q A G A W
N E B R S D I Y C N U R Q T C N B L X
I G N O M I N Y P N E M A T I C X L B
K B O P G V B P T I Z S L X T A V I Y Y
K S C I E E A U C P C F L A S S N E D T
P S O S S L E P N V V E N T S P H Z C R
T U R U T Y N B P D X I E Y S G H A Q
S B D B I T D C G A M T T L K L E Y J S
F V U L C I O H H U L A Y R U R W T O D
N E R I U N R Z R R L L S M I V L R L Z
D R E M L U S G K U O Q I D Z F A Y E T
P S R E A P E J T D J N L N P K I P R D
N I F F T M W S I Q O R I L G J T E Y T
Y V J L I I O O H U F H L C X Z S K D R
X E H L N P U J S U N A B A S H E D H F
S Z C Y G S F L A G R A N T L Y B X C N
```

About to die (8)
Anxiously (14)
Arousing a strong dislike or disgust (6)
Become unconditioned; revert back to old ways (11)
Bodily movements, particularly for communication of an idea or for emphasis (13)
Bodily waste; excrement (6)
Cliff (9)
Continual; recurring (7)
Disgrace (8)
Disgraceful; disdainful; scornful (12)
Enlightened; emitting light (8)
Exemption from punishment (8)
Filled with air (9)
Flabby; listless (7)
Give approval of or support to (7)
Hard outer covering (8)
Impressively great (10)
Indulging in excessive sexual activity (9)
Inherently; as a part of the nature of a thing itself (13)

Lacking reason and intellect (7)
Made to look like glass (9)
Meditating; thinking (10)
Most favorable point (8)
Mournful (9)
Multiply rapidly (11)
Noble; majestic; impressive (7)
Not disconcerted or embarrassed; calm (9)
Obviously; conspicuously (10)
Practice of being married to one person at a time (8)
Regret; remorse (11)
Rules or ideas that are taken for granted (10)
Self-evident; not needing proof (9)
Shocking (9)
Social class (5)
Thing of value (5)
Tirelessly (13)
Undecided (10)
Undermining; damaging to the authorities (10)
Urging with gentle and repeated appeals, teasing or flattery (8)

Brave New World Vocabulary Word Search 2 Answer Key

Words are placed backwards, forward, diagonally, up and down. Clues listed below can help you find the words. Circle the hidden vocabulary words in the maze.

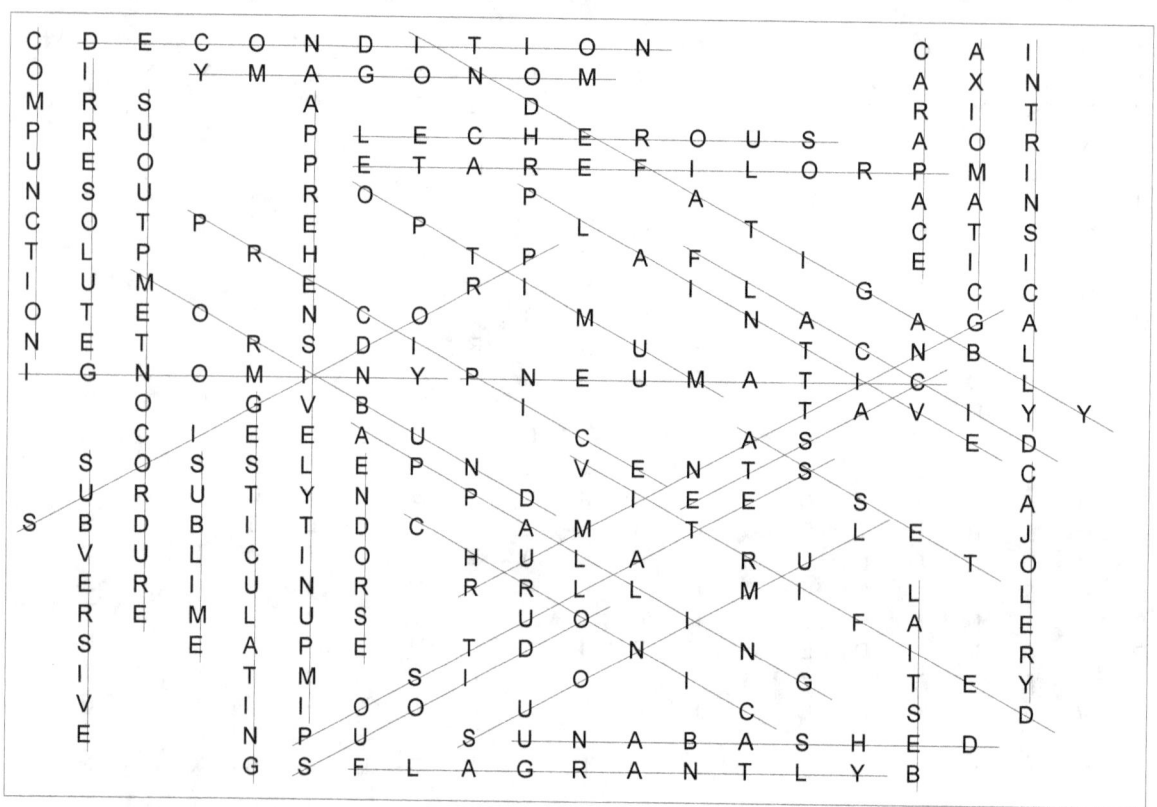

About to die (8)
Anxiously (14)
Arousing a strong dislike or disgust (6)
Become unconditioned; revert back to old ways (11)
Bodily movements, particularly for communication of an idea or for emphasis (13)
Bodily waste; excrement (6)
Cliff (9)
Continual; recurring (7)
Disgrace (8)
Disgraceful; disdainful; scornful (12)
Enlightened; emitting light (8)
Exemption from punishment (8)
Filled with air (9)
Flabby; listless (7)
Give approval of or support to (7)
Hard outer covering (8)
Impressively great (10)
Indulging in excessive sexual activity (9)
Inherently; as a part of the nature of a thing itself (13)

Lacking reason and intellect (7)
Made to look like glass (9)
Meditating; thinking (10)
Most favorable point (8)
Mournful (9)
Multiply rapidly (11)
Noble; majestic; impressive (7)
Not disconcerted or embarrassed; calm (9)
Obviously; conspicuously (10)
Practice of being married to one person at a time (8)
Regret; remorse (11)
Rules or ideas that are taken for granted (10)
Self-evident; not needing proof (9)
Shocking (9)
Social class (5)
Thing of value (5)
Tirelessly (13)
Undecided (10)
Undermining; damaging to the authorities (10)
Urging with gentle and repeated appeals, teasing or flattery (8)

Brave New World Vocabulary Word Search 3

Words are placed backwards, forward, diagonally, up and down. Words listed below are included in the maze. Circle the hidden vocabulary words in the maze.

```
X U N P R E C E D E N T E D H D N F C L
G I R N K M H V P N E U M A T I C M S L
B N E R H Z R I F C J O J C I S R H U J
R G M U P X O T S W N O F S N D H O O E
C R I M F J N N V O I H Z T T C C R N X
Q A L I C J I I G V V R B T R Y D D I H
Q T B N K O C A X Q T V R L I M O O M H
W I U A Y J M L P A W B V E N R N R U X
C A S T E Y A P P R E H E N S I V E L Y
A T E I R B Z P U S F C V E I O S Y L P
N I L N T E A D T N A R T F C R L F P T
N N B G F L C I T P C A R Y A E P U A N
I G A R L A A I A H L T M F L P R J T Y
H G T I A L S R P U L U I N L A O F R E
I B N G G N A S T R M D Y O Y R D R O F
L G U N R C J S E I O I P C N A I N F F
A L O O A P O Z T T F C G V C T G M I Y
T E M M N P C P M Q M C A I Y I I P Z L
I C R I T O O N B O T A B T R O O U I S
N H U N L D Q R R B M L P R E N U N G G
G E S Y Y I W I D D N F B I L D S I G M
R R N X B O B M Z B P W L F O S V T L T
C O I N D U L G E N T L Y I J H B Y Y Z
F U W S N S J K V M M N K E A G W Z Z B
M S X D A X I O M A T I C D C S Z W J N
```

ANNIHILATING   FLAGRANTLY   OPTIMUM

APPALLING   IGNOMINY   ORDURE

APPREHENSIVELY   IMPUNITY   PATRONIZINGLY

ASSET   INDULGENTLY   PLAINTIVE

AXIOMATIC   INGRATIATING   PNEUMATIC

BESTIAL   INSURMOUNTABLE   POSTULATES

CAJOLERY   INTRINSICALLY   PRODIGIOUS

CARAPACE   IRRESOLUTE   RECIPROCATED

CASTE   LECHEROUS   REPARATION

CHRONIC   LUMINOUS   RUMINATING

COMPUNCTION   MONOGAMY   SUBLIME

ENDORSE   MORIBUND   UNPRECEDENTED

FLACCID   ODIOUS   VITRIFIED

Copyrighted

Brave New World Vocabulary Word Search 3 Answer Key

Words are placed backwards, forward, diagonally, up and down. Words listed below are included in the maze. Circle the hidden vocabulary words in the maze.

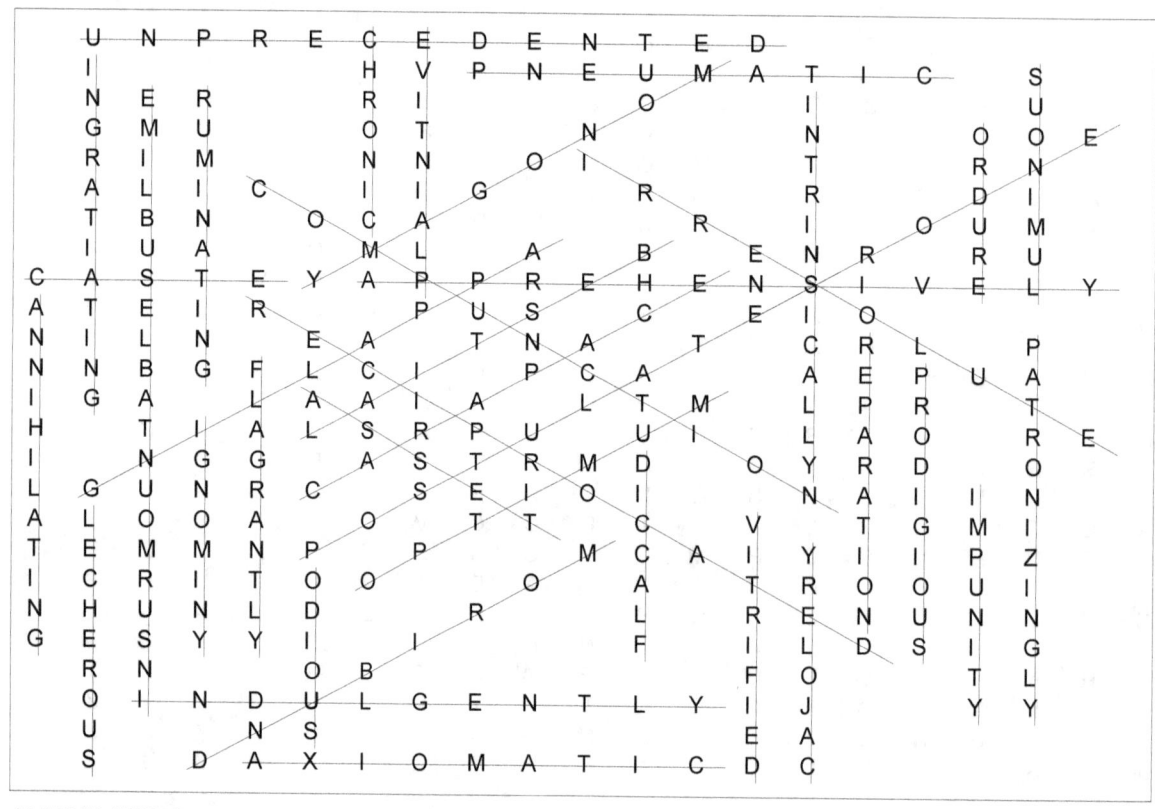

ANNIHILATING	FLAGRANTLY	OPTIMUM
APPALLING	IGNOMINY	ORDURE
APPREHENSIVELY	IMPUNITY	PATRONIZINGLY
ASSET	INDULGENTLY	PLAINTIVE
AXIOMATIC	INGRATIATING	PNEUMATIC
BESTIAL	INSURMOUNTABLE	POSTULATES
CAJOLERY	INTRINSICALLY	PRODIGIOUS
CARAPACE	IRRESOLUTE	RECIPROCATED
CASTE	LECHEROUS	REPARATION
CHRONIC	LUMINOUS	RUMINATING
COMPUNCTION	MONOGAMY	SUBLIME
ENDORSE	MORIBUND	UNPRECEDENTED
FLACCID	ODIOUS	VITRIFIED

Brave New World Vocabulary Word Search 4

Words are placed backwards, forward, diagonally, up and down. Words listed below are included in the maze. Circle the hidden vocabulary words in the maze.

```
I N D E F A T I G A B L Y K V P I C V W
Y M R W Y Y M T U D B H F D I R G O F X
L F P S L L M G N Y E M N S T O N F S N
B F L U T E E N A S N Y C R D O T C N J
I S M V N V V W B J E R B C I I M E W J
T Y N T E I I C A P V P V F F G I M E W
P K V X G S T T S X O W R F I I N P V K
E W G B L N N Y H B L S A V E O Y T I D
C C P Z U E I Z E D E N T O D U T U S V
R X J N D H A P D Z N S O P S B O R G
E U M T N E L D T I T O C D L T G U E A
P C M P I R P Q H D L R X I A I S V X
M B D I Z P B I L I Y D B V N O T M B I
I M B B N P L E W V R U H N Q I U E U O
C A R A P A C E S U O R E H C E L S S M
N C Y C T M T U N T P E E U H A D X S A
J N X I V O O I M Y I R L S R B S U Y T
Z F N T T N M K N L X A E N O R B T Z I
F G V A I O P O K G T N L C N L S Q E C
L X J M C G V R I F J S B I F U S T Y
A V U U D A W G N I P R C M C P R T R X
C L X E Y M N G W P B C E M Y O I V E P
C Y H N D Y A S S E T U M M D L F C H T
I R E P A R A T I O N W N N P Y S N E F
D C A J O L E R Y J M L E D W H P Q J V
```

ANNIHILATING
APPREHENSIVELY
ASSET
AXIOMATIC
BENEVOLENTLY
BESTIAL
CAJOLERY
CARAPACE
CASTE
CHRONIC
CONTEMPTUOUS
ENDORSE
FLACCID

GESTICULATING
IGNOMINY
IMPERCEPTIBLY
IMPUNITY
INDEFATIGABLY
INDULGENTLY
IRRESOLUTE
LECHEROUS
LUMINOUS
MONOGAMY
MORIBUND
ODIOUS
OPTIMUM

ORDURE
PLAINTIVE
PNEUMATIC
POSTULATES
PRECIPICE
PRODIGIOUS
REPARATION
RUMINATING
SUBLIME
SUBVERSIVE
UNABASHED
VITRIFIED

Brave New World Vocabulary Word Search 4 Answer Key

Words are placed backwards, forward, diagonally, up and down. Words listed below are included in the maze. Circle the hidden vocabulary words in the maze.

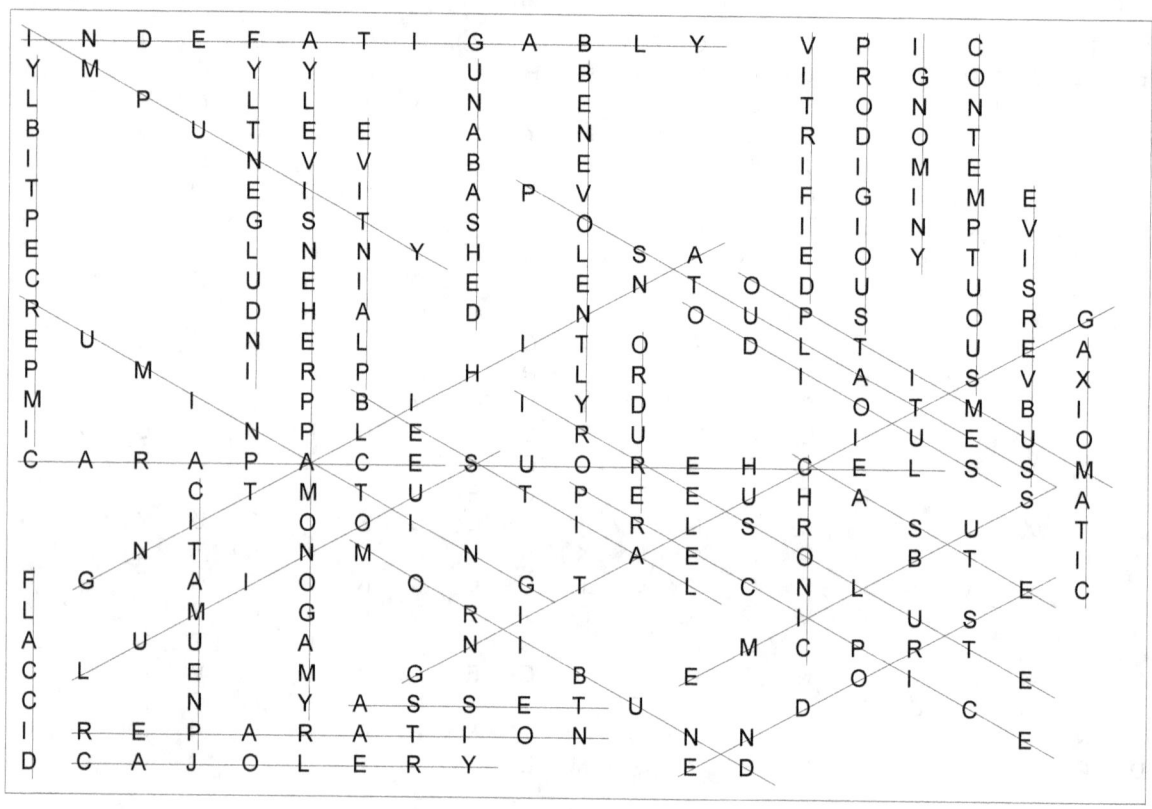

ANNIHILATING	GESTICULATING	ORDURE
APPREHENSIVELY	IGNOMINY	PLAINTIVE
ASSET	IMPERCEPTIBLY	PNEUMATIC
AXIOMATIC	IMPUNITY	POSTULATES
BENEVOLENTLY	INDEFATIGABLY	PRECIPICE
BESTIAL	INDULGENTLY	PRODIGIOUS
CAJOLERY	IRRESOLUTE	REPARATION
CARAPACE	LECHEROUS	RUMINATING
CASTE	LUMINOUS	SUBLIME
CHRONIC	MONOGAMY	SUBVERSIVE
CONTEMPTUOUS	MORIBUND	UNABASHED
ENDORSE	ODIOUS	VITRIFIED
FLACCID	OPTIMUM	

Brave New World Vocabulary Crossword 1

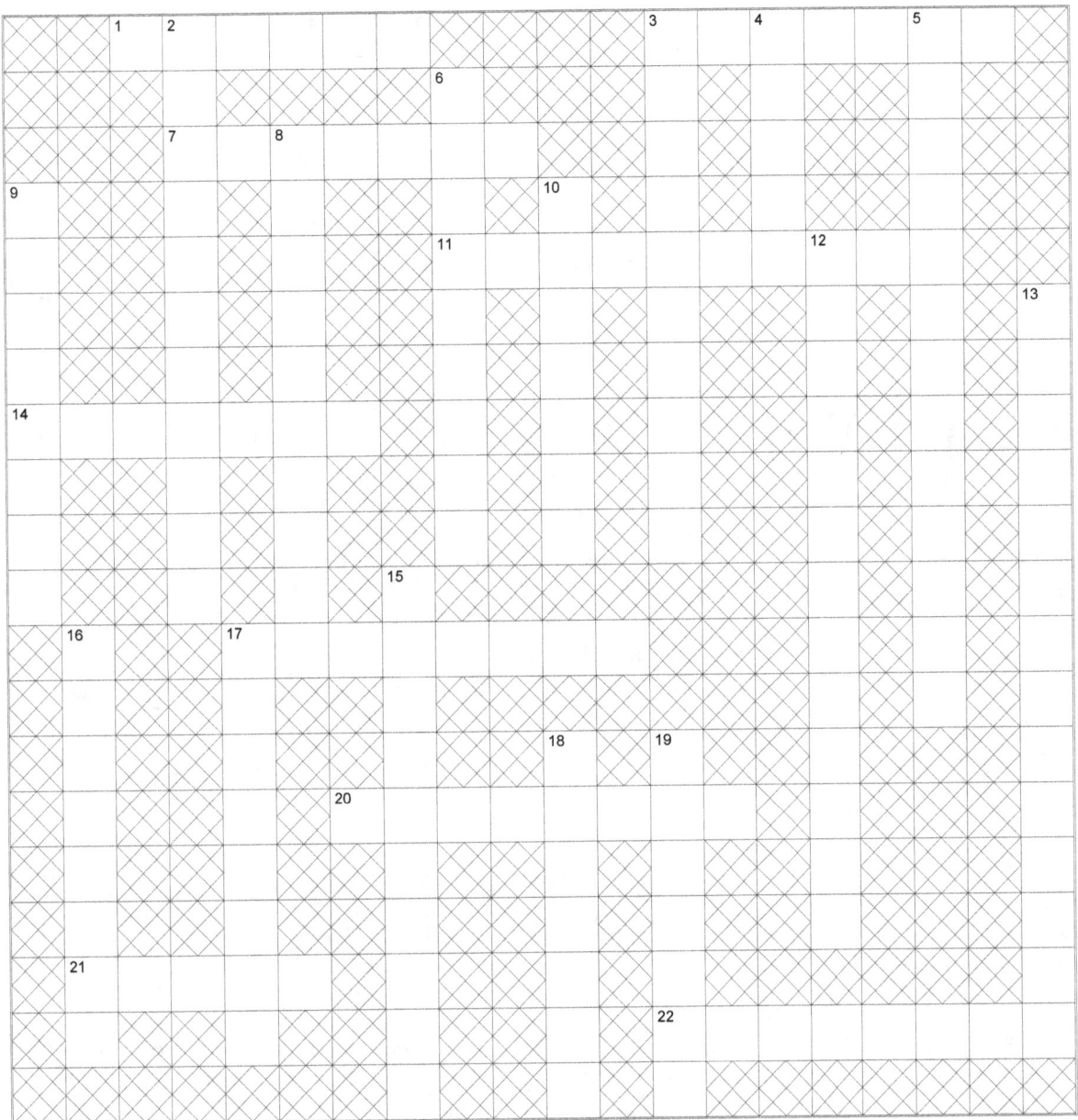

Across
1. Arousing a strong dislike or disgust
3. Flabby; listless
7. Continual; recurring
11. Compensation; something to make amends
14. Lacking reason and intellect
17. Disgrace
20. Enlightened; emitting light
21. Social class
22. Practice of being married to one person at a time

Down
2. Become unconditioned; revert back to old ways
3. Obviously; conspicuously
4. Thing of value
5. Unbelievable
6. Made to look like glass
8. Meditating; thinking
9. About to die
10. Most favorable point
12. Inherently; as a part of the nature of a thing itself
13. Anxiously
15. Rules or ideas that are taken for granted
16. Hard outer covering
17. Exemption from punishment
18. Give approval of or support to
19. Noble; majestic; impressive

Brave New World Vocabulary Crossword 1 Answer Key

Across
1. Arousing a strong dislike or disgust
3. Flabby; listless
7. Continual; recurring
11. Compensation; something to make amends
14. Lacking reason and intellect
17. Disgrace
20. Enlightened; emitting light
21. Social class
22. Practice of being married to one person at a time

Down
2. Become unconditioned; revert back to old ways
3. Obviously; conspicuously
4. Thing of value
5. Unbelievable
6. Made to look like glass
8. Meditating; thinking
9. About to die
10. Most favorable point
12. Inherently; as a part of the nature of a thing itself
13. Anxiously
15. Rules or ideas that are taken for granted
16. Hard outer covering
17. Exemption from punishment
18. Give approval of or support to
19. Noble; majestic; impressive

Brave New World Vocabulary Crossword 2

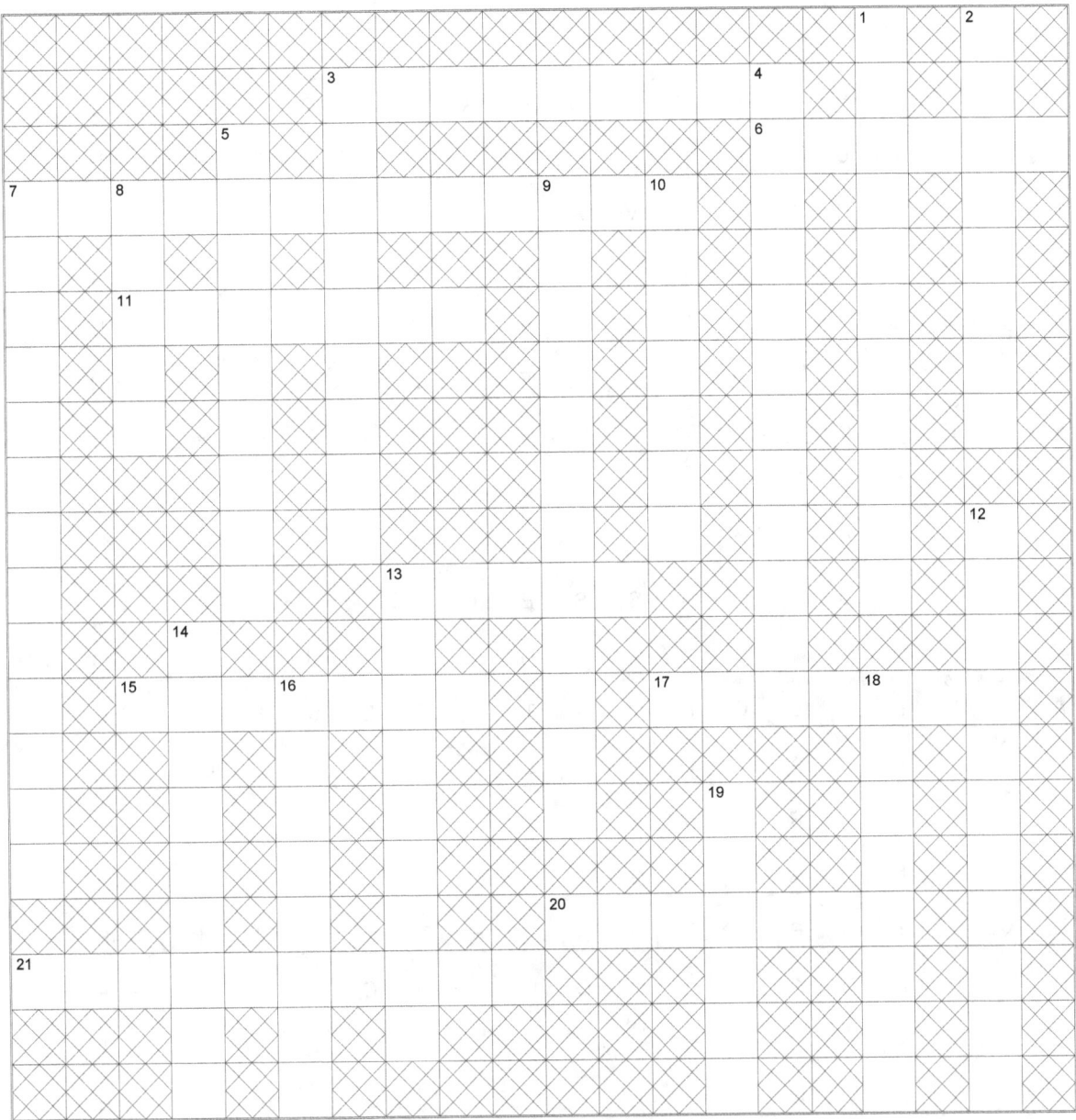

Across
3. Filled with air
6. Bodily waste; excrement
7. Unbelievable
11. Noble; majestic; impressive
13. Thing of value
15. Flabby; listless
17. Lacking reason and intellect
20. Most favorable point
21. Meditating; thinking

Down
1. As if doing one a favor
2. About to die
3. Cliff
4. Disgraceful; disdainful; scornful
5. Not disconcerted or embarrassed; calm
7. Inherently; as a part of the nature of a thing itself
8. Social class
9. Harmlessly; in a beneficial way
10. Give approval of or support to
12. Multiply rapidly
13. Self-evident; not needing proof
14. Mournful
16. Hard outer covering
18. Disgrace
19. Arousing a strong dislike or disgust

Brave New World Vocabulary Crossword 2 Answer Key

Across
3. Filled with air
6. Bodily waste; excrement
7. Unbelievable
11. Noble; majestic; impressive
13. Thing of value
15. Flabby; listless
17. Lacking reason and intellect
20. Most favorable point
21. Meditating; thinking

Down
1. As if doing one a favor
2. About to die
3. Cliff
4. Disgraceful; disdainful; scornful
5. Not disconcerted or embarrassed; calm
7. Inherently; as a part of the nature of a thing itself
8. Social class
9. Harmlessly; in a beneficial way
10. Give approval of or support to
12. Multiply rapidly
13. Self-evident; not needing proof
14. Mournful
16. Hard outer covering
18. Disgrace
19. Arousing a strong dislike or disgust

Copyrighted

Brave New World Vocabulary Crossword 3

Across
1. Lacking reason and intellect
2. Most favorable point
4. Exemption from punishment
5. Cliff
8. Give approval of or support to
9. Social class
11. About to die
13. Flabby; listless
15. Made to look like glass
18. Noble; majestic; impressive
19. Having never happened before
20. Thing of value
21. Indulging in excessive sexual activity

Down
1. Harmlessly; in a beneficial way
2. Arousing a strong dislike or disgust
3. Practice of being married to one person at a time
5. Rules or ideas that are taken for granted
6. Filled with air
7. Become unconditioned; revert back to old ways
10. Disgraceful; disdainful; scornful
12. Inherently; as a part of the nature of a thing itself
14. Self-evident; not needing proof
16. Bodily waste; excrement
17. Continual; recurring

Brave New World Vocabulary Crossword 3 Answer Key

Across
1. Lacking reason and intellect
2. Most favorable point
4. Exemption from punishment
5. Cliff
8. Give approval of or support to
9. Social class
11. About to die
13. Flabby; listless
15. Made to look like glass
18. Noble; majestic; impressive
19. Having never happened before
20. Thing of value
21. Indulging in excessive sexual activity

Down
1. Harmlessly; in a beneficial way
2. Arousing a strong dislike or disgust
3. Practice of being married to one person at a time
5. Rules or ideas that are taken for granted
6. Filled with air
7. Become unconditioned; revert back to old ways
10. Disgraceful; disdainful; scornful
12. Inherently; as a part of the nature of a thing itself
14. Self-evident; not needing proof
16. Bodily waste; excrement
17. Continual; recurring

Brave New World Vocabulary Crossword 4

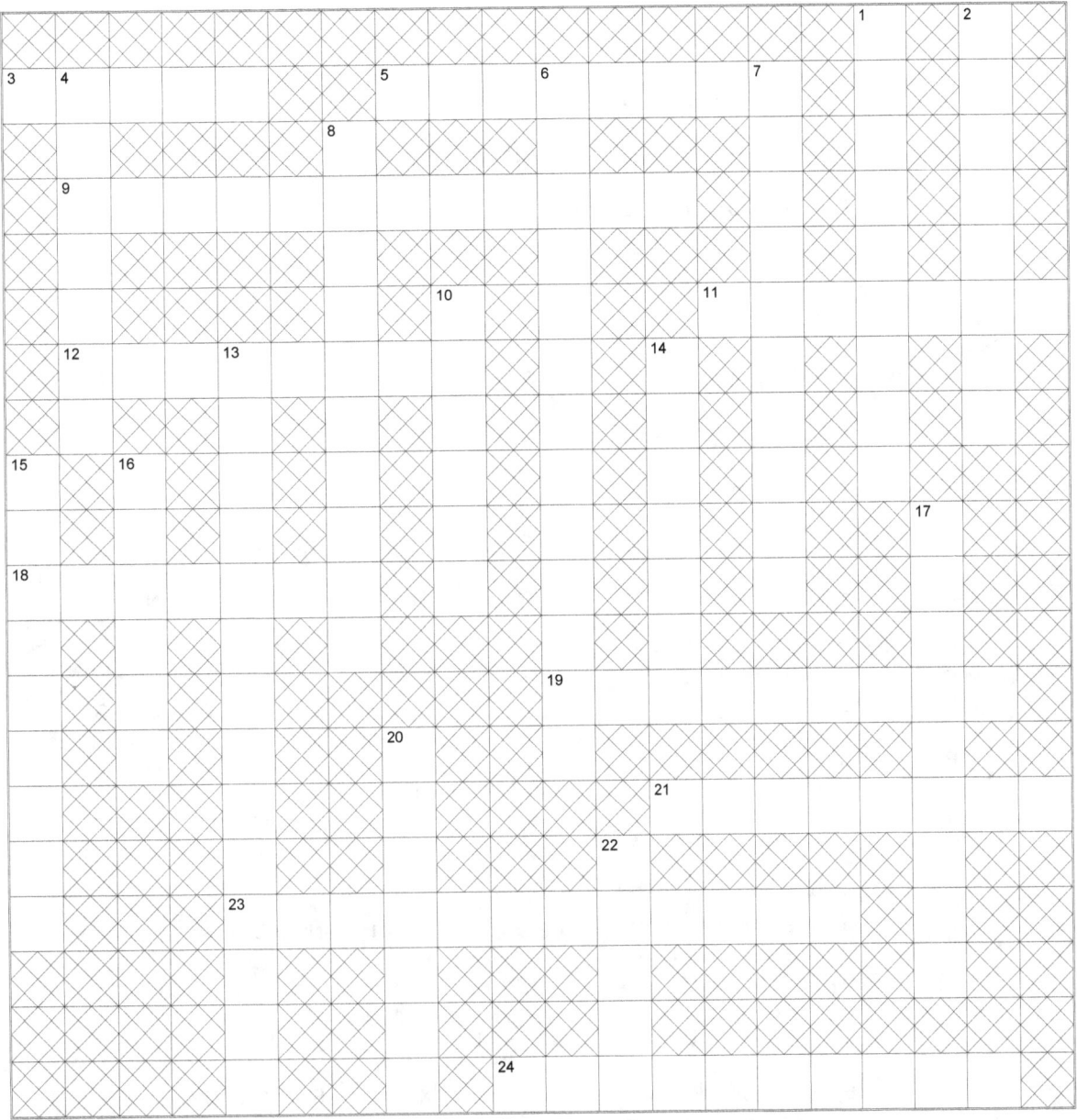

Across
3. Thing of value
5. Enlightened; emitting light
9. Harmlessly; in a beneficial way
11. Lacking reason and intellect
12. About to die
18. Give approval of or support to
19. Indulging in excessive sexual activity
21. Practice of being married to one person at a time
23. Completely overwhelming or incapacitating
24. Relentlessly; without stopping

Down
1. Mournful
2. Hard outer covering
4. Noble; majestic; impressive
6. Inherently; as a part of the nature of a thing itself
7. Undermining; damaging to the authorities
8. Rules or ideas that are taken for granted
10. Arousing a strong dislike or disgust
13. Impossible to overcome
14. Continual; recurring
15. Cliff
16. Bodily waste; excrement
17. Filled with air
20. Most favorable point
22. Social class

Brave New World Vocabulary Crossword 4 Answer Key

Across
3. Thing of value
5. Enlightened; emitting light
9. Harmlessly; in a beneficial way
11. Lacking reason and intellect
12. About to die
18. Give approval of or support to
19. Indulging in excessive sexual activity
21. Practice of being married to one person at a time
23. Completely overwhelming or incapacitating
24. Relentlessly; without stopping

Down
1. Mournful
2. Hard outer covering
4. Noble; majestic; impressive
6. Inherently; as a part of the nature of a thing itself
7. Undermining; damaging to the authorities
8. Rules or ideas that are taken for granted
10. Arousing a strong dislike or disgust
13. Impossible to overcome
14. Continual; recurring
15. Cliff
16. Bodily waste; excrement
17. Filled with air
20. Most favorable point
22. Social class

Brave New World Vocabulary Juggle Letters 1

1. OMMNYGOA = 1. _____
   Practice of being married to one person at a time

2. NHPTALEEIRTYACL = 2. _____
   As if in parentheses; aside

3. IPPCEREIC = 3. _____
   Cliff

4. UIPDOSOGIR = 4. _____
   Impressively great

5. ZPRIOLGIAYNNT = 5. _____
   In a condescending manner

6. TOLTPESUSA = 6. _____
   Rules or ideas that are taken for granted

7. TIFALRPOREE = 7. _____
   Multiply rapidly

8. AIGGTCNEUSITL = 8. _____
   Bodily movements, particularly for communication of an idea or for emphasis

9. BLENORAIYX = 9. _____
   Relentlessly; without stopping

10. ETRCDCIREPAO = 10. _____
    Returned; mutually shared

11. EIRCMIBEPPYLT = 11. _____
    Unable to be detected by the senses

12. ISLMUNOU = 12. _____
    Enlightened; emitting light

13. NNETYUILLGD = 13. _____
    As if doing one a favor

14. REECDNEDTNEPU = 14. _____
    Having never happened before

15. OIHCRCN = 15. _____
    Continual; recurring

Brave New World Vocabulary Juggle Letters 1 Answer Key

1. OMMNYGOA = 1. MONOGAMY
   Practice of being married to one person at a time

2. NHPTALEEIRTYACL = 2. PARENTHETICALLY
   As if in parentheses; aside

3. IPPCEREIC = 3. PRECIPICE
   Cliff

4. UIPDOSOGIR = 4. PRODIGIOUS
   Impressively great

5. ZPRIOLGIAYNNT = 5. PATRONIZINGLY
   In a condescending manner

6. TOLTPESUSA = 6. POSTULATES
   Rules or ideas that are taken for granted

7. TIFALRPOREE = 7. PROLIFERATE
   Multiply rapidly

8. AIGGTCNEUSITL = 8. GESTICULATING
   Bodily movements, particularly for communication of an idea or for emphasis

9. BLENORAIYX = 9. INEXORABLY
   Relentlessly; without stopping

10. ETRCDCIREPAO = 10. RECIPROCATED
    Returned; mutually shared

11. EIRCMIBEPPYLT = 11. IMPERCEPTIBLY
    Unable to be detected by the senses

12. ISLMUNOU = 12. LUMINOUS
    Enlightened; emitting light

13. NNETYUILLGD = 13. INDULGENTLY
    As if doing one a favor

14. REECDNEDTNEPU = 14. UNPRECEDENTED
    Having never happened before

15. OIHCRCN = 15. CHRONIC
    Continual; recurring

Brave New World Vocabulary Juggle Letters 2

1. RHUOECLES = 1. _____
   Indulging in excessive sexual activity

2. LAOEYRCJ = 2. _____
   Urging with gentle and repeated appeals, teasing or flattery

3. UPITMNIY = 3. _____
   Exemption from punishment

4. EORFARTELPI = 4. _____
   Multiply rapidly

5. AYTFANGRLL = 5. _____
   Obviously; conspicuously

6. TNUAMGRIIN = 6. _____
   Meditating; thinking

7. SLETUSATPO = 7. _____
   Rules or ideas that are taken for granted

8. NAFIBTDEYLGIA = 8. _____
   Tirelessly

9. ALIEEBINCNVCO = 9. _____
   Unbelievable

10. RSEENDO = 10. _____
    Give approval of or support to

11. GATNIRITAIGN = 11. _____
    Making oneself favorable to another

12. CIAFLCD = 12. _____
    Flabby; listless

13. TNOLLYNVBEEE = 13. _____
    Harmlessly; in a beneficial way

14. NNINIIHAGLAT = 14. _____
    Completely overwhelming or incapacitating

15. NNGTDELILUY = 15. _____
    As if doing one a favor

Brave New World Vocabulary Juggle Letters 2 Answer Key

1. RHUOECLES = 1. LECHEROUS
Indulging in excessive sexual activity

2. LAOEYRCJ = 2. CAJOLERY
Urging with gentle and repeated appeals, teasing or flattery

3. UPITMNIY = 3. IMPUNITY
Exemption from punishment

4. EORFARTELPI = 4. PROLIFERATE
Multiply rapidly

5. AYTFANGRLL = 5. FLAGRANTLY
Obviously; conspicuously

6. TNUAMGRIIN = 6. RUMINATING
Meditating; thinking

7. SLETUSATPO = 7. POSTULATES
Rules or ideas that are taken for granted

8. NAFIBTDEYLGIA = 8. INDEFATIGABLY
Tirelessly

9. ALIEEBINCNVCO = 9. INCONCEIVABLE
Unbelievable

10. RSEENDO = 10. ENDORSE
Give approval of or support to

11. GATNIRITAIGN = 11. INGRATIATING
Making oneself favorable to another

12. CIAFLCD = 12. FLACCID
Flabby; listless

13. TNOLLYNVBEEE = 13. BENEVOLENTLY
Harmlessly; in a beneficial way

14. NNINIIHAGLAT = 14. ANNIHILATING
Completely overwhelming or incapacitating

15. NNGTDELILUY = 15. INDULGENTLY
As if doing one a favor

Brave New World Vocabulary Juggle Letters 3

1. ISDUOO = 1. _____
Arousing a strong dislike or disgust

2. EESORND = 2. _____
Give approval of or support to

3. OEJACRYL = 3. _____
Urging with gentle and repeated appeals, teasing or flattery

4. ELSEOHURC = 4. _____
Indulging in excessive sexual activity

5. INDTEDIONCO = 5. _____
Become unconditioned; revert back to old ways

6. UEOPSTLSTA = 6. _____
Rules or ideas that are taken for granted

7. PIEMATUCN = 7. _____
Filled with air

8. OCRHCIN = 8. _____
Continual; recurring

9. LSIBETA = 9. _____
Lacking reason and intellect

10. EERFLRAOTPI =10. _____
Multiply rapidly

11. PCIECRPIE =11. _____
Cliff

12. ILEINAPVT =12. _____
Mournful

13. LPALAGPNI =13. _____
Shocking

14. ESATC =14. _____
Social class

15. SASET =15. _____
Thing of value

Brave New World Vocabulary Juggle Letters 3 Answer Key

1. ISDUOO = 1. ODIOUS
Arousing a strong dislike or disgust

2. EESORND = 2. ENDORSE
Give approval of or support to

3. OEJACRYL = 3. CAJOLERY
Urging with gentle and repeated appeals, teasing or flattery

4. ELSEOHURC = 4. LECHEROUS
Indulging in excessive sexual activity

5. INDTEDIONCO = 5. DECONDITION
Become unconditioned; revert back to old ways

6. UEOPSTLSTA = 6. POSTULATES
Rules or ideas that are taken for granted

7. PIEMATUCN = 7. PNEUMATIC
Filled with air

8. OCRHCIN = 8. CHRONIC
Continual; recurring

9. LSIBETA = 9. BESTIAL
Lacking reason and intellect

10. EERFLRAOTPI =10. PROLIFERATE
Multiply rapidly

11. PCIECRPIE =11. PRECIPICE
Cliff

12. ILEINAPVT =12. PLAINTIVE
Mournful

13. LPALAGPNI =13. APPALLING
Shocking

14. ESATC =14. CASTE
Social class

15. SASET =15. ASSET
Thing of value

Brave New World Vocabulary Juggle Letters 4

1. EEBVOLNLTNEY = 1. _____
   Harmlessly; in a beneficial way

2. GNULLYEITDN = 2. _____
   As if doing one a favor

3. PECARCAA = 3. _____
   Hard outer covering

4. HLTINAANIIGN = 4. _____
   Completely overwhelming or incapacitating

5. HINCOCR = 5. _____
   Continual; recurring

6. MOSLUUNI = 6. _____
   Enlightened; emitting light

7. ETASS = 7. _____
   Thing of value

8. IEDNIOTONDC = 8. _____
   Become unconditioned; revert back to old ways

9. ABITSEL = 9. _____
   Lacking reason and intellect

10. TTOESSAULP =10. _____
    Rules or ideas that are taken for granted

11. LCFCAID =11. _____
    Flabby; listless

12. TNTRANGIGIIA =12. _____
    Making oneself favorable to another

13. DVRETIFII =13. _____
    Made to look like glass

14. ANEIVPITL =14. _____
    Mournful

15. FRELOPAEITR =15. _____
    Multiply rapidly

Brave New World Vocabulary Juggle Letters 4 Answer Key

1. EEBVOLNLTNEY = 1. BENEVOLENTLY
   Harmlessly; in a beneficial way

2. GNULLYEITDN = 2. INDULGENTLY
   As if doing one a favor

3. PECARCAA = 3. CARAPACE
   Hard outer covering

4. HLTINAANIIGN = 4. ANNIHILATING
   Completely overwhelming or incapacitating

5. HINCOCR = 5. CHRONIC
   Continual; recurring

6. MOSLUUNI = 6. LUMINOUS
   Enlightened; emitting light

7. ETASS = 7. ASSET
   Thing of value

8. IEDNIOTONDC = 8. DECONDITION
   Become unconditioned; revert back to old ways

9. ABITSEL = 9. BESTIAL
   Lacking reason and intellect

10. TTOESSAULP =10. POSTULATES
    Rules or ideas that are taken for granted

11. LCFCAID =11. FLACCID
    Flabby; listless

12. TNTRANGIGIIA =12. INGRATIATING
    Making oneself favorable to another

13. DVRETIFII =13. VITRIFIED
    Made to look like glass

14. ANEIVPITL =14. PLAINTIVE
    Mournful

15. FRELOPAEITR =15. PROLIFERATE
    Multiply rapidly

ANNIHILATING	Completely overwhelming or incapacitating
APPALLING	Shocking
APPREHENSIVELY	Anxiously
ASSET	Thing of value
AXIOMATIC	Self-evident; not needing proof
BENEVOLENTLY	Harmlessly; in a beneficial way

BESTIAL	Lacking reason and intellect
CAJOLERY	Urging with gentle and repeated appeals, teasing or flattery
CARAPACE	Hard outer covering
CASTE	Social class
CHRONIC	Continual; recurring
COMPUNCTION	Regret; remorse

CONTEMPTUOUS	Disgraceful; disdainful; scornful
DECONDITION	Become unconditioned; revert back to old ways
ENDORSE	Give approval of or support to
FLACCID	Flabby; listless
FLAGRANTLY	Obviously; conspicuously
GESTICULATING	Bodily movements, particularly for communication of an idea or for emphasis

IGNOMINY	Disgrace
IMPERCEPTIBLY	Unable to be detected by the senses
IMPUNITY	Exemption from punishment
INCONCEIVABLE	Unbelievable
INDEFATIGABLY	Tirelessly
INDULGENTLY	As if doing one a favor

INEXORABLY	Relentlessly; without stopping
INGRATIATING	Making oneself favorable to another
INSURMOUNTABLE	Impossible to overcome
INTRINSICALLY	Inherently; as a part of the nature of a thing itself
IRRESOLUTE	Undecided
LECHEROUS	Indulging in excessive sexual activity

LUMINOUS	Enlightened; emitting light
MONOGAMY	Practice of being married to one person at a time
MORIBUND	About to die
ODIOUS	Arousing a strong dislike or disgust
OPTIMUM	Most favorable point
ORDURE	Bodily waste; excrement

PARENTHETICALLY	As if in parentheses; aside
PATRONIZINGLY	In a condescending manner
PLAINTIVE	Mournful
PNEUMATIC	Filled with air
POSTULATES	Rules or ideas that are taken for granted
PRECIPICE	Cliff

PRODIGIOUS	Impressively great
PROLIFERATE	Multiply rapidly
RECIPROCATED	Returned; mutually shared
REPARATION	Compensation; something to make amends
RUMINATING	Meditating; thinking
SUBLIME	Noble; majestic; impressive

SUBVERSIVE	Undermining; damaging to the authorities
UNABASHED	Not disconcerted or embarrassed; calm
UNPRECEDENTED	Having never happened before
VITRIFIED	Made to look like glass

Brave New World Vocabulary

LUMINOUS	REPARATION	AXIOMATIC	LECHEROUS	APPALLING
DECONDITION	PATRONIZINGLY	CHRONIC	CASTE	FLACCID
INTRINSICALLY	POSTULATES	FREE SPACE	OPTIMUM	INDULGENTLY
RECIPROCATED	SUBVERSIVE	IMPUNITY	ORDURE	INCONCEIVABLE
INSURMOUNTABLE	PROLIFERATE	RUMINATING	UNABASHED	MORIBUND

Brave New World Vocabulary

PRODIGIOUS	IMPERCEPTIBLY	PLAINTIVE	COMPUNCTION	CONTEMPTUOUS
INGRATIATING	ANNIHILATING	CAJOLERY	PRECIPICE	SUBLIME
BESTIAL	PARENTHETICALLY	FREE SPACE	IGNOMINY	APPREHENSIVELY
ODIOUS	VITRIFIED	GESTICULATING	ASSET	PNEUMATIC
INEXORABLY	BENEVOLENTLY	FLAGRANTLY	UNPRECEDENTED	IRRESOLUTE

Brave New World Vocabulary

INDULGENTLY	ODIOUS	PROLIFERATE	APPALLING	IMPERCEPTIBLY
LUMINOUS	COMPUNCTION	ENDORSE	INTRINSICALLY	PATRONIZINGLY
UNPRECEDENTED	CHRONIC	FREE SPACE	CONTEMPTUOUS	LECHEROUS
MORIBUND	RECIPROCATED	GESTICULATING	INDEFATIGABLY	OPTIMUM
PRODIGIOUS	ASSET	PRECIPICE	BENEVOLENTLY	DECONDITION

Brave New World Vocabulary

ANNIHILATING	PNEUMATIC	UNABASHED	APPREHENSIVELY	CAJOLERY
SUBVERSIVE	IMPUNITY	RUMINATING	REPARATION	BESTIAL
IRRESOLUTE	INCONCEIVABLE	FREE SPACE	SUBLIME	FLAGRANTLY
INGRATIATING	PLAINTIVE	POSTULATES	AXIOMATIC	VITRIFIED
ORDURE	PARENTHETICALLY	INSURMOUNTABLE	CARAPACE	IGNOMINY

Brave New World Vocabulary

APPALLING	FLAGRANTLY	CHRONIC	CARAPACE	ENDORSE
RECIPROCATED	CAJOLERY	INTRINSICALLY	CASTE	ORDURE
LUMINOUS	BENEVOLENTLY	FREE SPACE	IRRESOLUTE	MONOGAMY
APPREHENSIVELY	INCONCEIVABLE	ANNIHILATING	VITRIFIED	FLACCID
IMPERCEPTIBLY	COMPUNCTION	INGRATIATING	PLAINTIVE	GESTICULATING

Brave New World Vocabulary

POSTULATES	PARENTHETICALLY	ASSET	INSURMOUNTABLE	AXIOMATIC
INDULGENTLY	SUBVERSIVE	IGNOMINY	IMPUNITY	LECHEROUS
PRECIPICE	INDEFATIGABLY	FREE SPACE	SUBLIME	PNEUMATIC
PATRONIZINGLY	ODIOUS	REPARATION	CONTEMPTUOUS	UNABASHED
UNPRECEDENTED	RUMINATING	DECONDITION	PROLIFERATE	BESTIAL

Brave New World Vocabulary

VITRIFIED	IMPERCEPTIBLY	INCONCEIVABLE	INTRINSICALLY	ASSET
AXIOMATIC	GESTICULATING	INEXORABLY	MONOGAMY	UNABASHED
IRRESOLUTE	PNEUMATIC	FREE SPACE	INSURMOUNTABLE	REPARATION
CAJOLERY	COMPUNCTION	ENDORSE	INDULGENTLY	BENEVOLENTLY
SUBVERSIVE	PRODIGIOUS	RECIPROCATED	PRECIPICE	CONTEMPTUOUS

Brave New World Vocabulary

ANNIHILATING	LECHEROUS	PLAINTIVE	IGNOMINY	MORIBUND
IMPUNITY	CASTE	CHRONIC	INDEFATIGABLY	DECONDITION
RUMINATING	BESTIAL	FREE SPACE	ORDURE	UNPRECEDENTED
FLACCID	APPREHENSIVELY	CARAPACE	FLAGRANTLY	INGRATIATING
PATRONIZINGLY	PARENTHETICALLY	LUMINOUS	PROLIFERATE	SUBLIME

Brave New World Vocabulary

GESTICULATING	FLAGRANTLY	CONTEMPTUOUS	POSTULATES	RUMINATING
INSURMOUNTABLE	BESTIAL	CAJOLERY	SUBLIME	CHRONIC
ASSET	PRECIPICE	FREE SPACE	INDULGENTLY	RECIPROCATED
ORDURE	PLAINTIVE	BENEVOLENTLY	IMPERCEPTIBLY	CARAPACE
INCONCEIVABLE	PROLIFERATE	AXIOMATIC	PNEUMATIC	PRODIGIOUS

Brave New World Vocabulary

ODIOUS	CASTE	IRRESOLUTE	MONOGAMY	IMPUNITY
APPALLING	UNPRECEDENTED	VITRIFIED	INEXORABLY	UNABASHED
PATRONIZINGLY	INGRATIATING	FREE SPACE	INDEFATIGABLY	OPTIMUM
PARENTHETICALLY	COMPUNCTION	LECHEROUS	IGNOMINY	REPARATION
FLACCID	INTRINSICALLY	APPREHENSIVELY	ANNIHILATING	SUBVERSIVE

Brave New World Vocabulary

MONOGAMY	FLAGRANTLY	PRECIPICE	INEXORABLY	PRODIGIOUS
RUMINATING	UNABASHED	INTRINSICALLY	ENDORSE	CASTE
REPARATION	POSTULATES	FREE SPACE	MORIBUND	PATRONIZINGLY
LECHEROUS	OPTIMUM	APPALLING	APPREHENSIVELY	AXIOMATIC
UNPRECEDENTED	COMPUNCTION	ORDURE	IRRESOLUTE	ANNIHILATING

Brave New World Vocabulary

INDULGENTLY	IMPUNITY	BESTIAL	FLACCID	INDEFATIGABLY
IMPERCEPTIBLY	CONTEMPTUOUS	ASSET	DECONDITION	VITRIFIED
CHRONIC	SUBVERSIVE	FREE SPACE	PNEUMATIC	PLAINTIVE
PARENTHETICALLY	CARAPACE	SUBLIME	INGRATIATING	INCONCEIVABLE
BENEVOLENTLY	ODIOUS	PROLIFERATE	RECIPROCATED	IGNOMINY

Brave New World Vocabulary

INEXORABLY	PARENTHETICALLY	PROLIFERATE	CASTE	IGNOMINY
CAJOLERY	CONTEMPTUOUS	PATRONIZINGLY	ORDURE	CHRONIC
PRODIGIOUS	PRECIPICE	FREE SPACE	INCONCEIVABLE	OPTIMUM
APPREHENSIVELY	SUBLIME	BESTIAL	COMPUNCTION	ODIOUS
FLAGRANTLY	MONOGAMY	FLACCID	INGRATIATING	IRRESOLUTE

Brave New World Vocabulary

POSTULATES	INDULGENTLY	IMPERCEPTIBLY	GESTICULATING	APPALLING
ANNIHILATING	INSURMOUNTABLE	MORIBUND	UNPRECEDENTED	RECIPROCATED
ASSET	PNEUMATIC	FREE SPACE	PLAINTIVE	LUMINOUS
CARAPACE	LECHEROUS	IMPUNITY	VITRIFIED	DECONDITION
BENEVOLENTLY	RUMINATING	SUBVERSIVE	REPARATION	ENDORSE

Brave New World Vocabulary

PARENTHETICALLY	INDEFATIGABLY	FLACCID	INCONCEIVABLE	CASTE
CARAPACE	LECHEROUS	VITRIFIED	IMPUNITY	INDULGENTLY
RECIPROCATED	SUBLIME	FREE SPACE	RUMINATING	FLAGRANTLY
BENEVOLENTLY	ENDORSE	OPTIMUM	SUBVERSIVE	POSTULATES
INTRINSICALLY	PRECIPICE	REPARATION	INGRATIATING	AXIOMATIC

Brave New World Vocabulary

ODIOUS	ASSET	APPREHENSIVELY	COMPUNCTION	MORIBUND
PROLIFERATE	IRRESOLUTE	PLAINTIVE	GESTICULATING	CAJOLERY
INSURMOUNTABLE	IGNOMINY	FREE SPACE	INEXORABLY	IMPERCEPTIBLY
BESTIAL	MONOGAMY	DECONDITION	UNPRECEDENTED	LUMINOUS
PRODIGIOUS	APPALLING	ORDURE	ANNIHILATING	PNEUMATIC

Brave New World Vocabulary

PNEUMATIC	SUBVERSIVE	MONOGAMY	LECHEROUS	PLAINTIVE
PRODIGIOUS	BENEVOLENTLY	ANNIHILATING	IMPERCEPTIBLY	REPARATION
RUMINATING	INDULGENTLY	FREE SPACE	AXIOMATIC	FLACCID
CAJOLERY	PATRONIZINGLY	ORDURE	IRRESOLUTE	ASSET
CHRONIC	UNABASHED	CASTE	ODIOUS	APPALLING

Brave New World Vocabulary

INSURMOUNTABLE	BESTIAL	DECONDITION	PARENTHETICALLY	INGRATIATING
ENDORSE	PRECIPICE	RECIPROCATED	COMPUNCTION	VITRIFIED
UNPRECEDENTED	OPTIMUM	FREE SPACE	INTRINSICALLY	POSTULATES
MORIBUND	LUMINOUS	INDEFATIGABLY	CONTEMPTUOUS	IMPUNITY
IGNOMINY	FLAGRANTLY	PROLIFERATE	APPREHENSIVELY	INEXORABLY

Brave New World Vocabulary

IGNOMINY	BENEVOLENTLY	OPTIMUM	SUBLIME	UNABASHED
FLACCID	INEXORABLY	IMPUNITY	UNPRECEDENTED	GESTICULATING
ANNIHILATING	PNEUMATIC	FREE SPACE	AXIOMATIC	LECHEROUS
CAJOLERY	APPREHENSIVELY	CARAPACE	ODIOUS	DECONDITION
ENDORSE	RUMINATING	MONOGAMY	APPALLING	ORDURE

Brave New World Vocabulary

RECIPROCATED	FLAGRANTLY	PRECIPICE	IMPERCEPTIBLY	ASSET
INDULGENTLY	LUMINOUS	SUBVERSIVE	PRODIGIOUS	VITRIFIED
REPARATION	IRRESOLUTE	FREE SPACE	BESTIAL	MORIBUND
PATRONIZINGLY	PLAINTIVE	CONTEMPTUOUS	POSTULATES	COMPUNCTION
CASTE	INTRINSICALLY	PARENTHETICALLY	INSURMOUNTABLE	PROLIFERATE

Brave New World Vocabulary

REPARATION	IRRESOLUTE	BESTIAL	RUMINATING	BENEVOLENTLY
INSURMOUNTABLE	MONOGAMY	PRODIGIOUS	INDULGENTLY	CHRONIC
FLACCID	LUMINOUS	FREE SPACE	UNABASHED	PROLIFERATE
IMPERCEPTIBLY	LECHEROUS	PATRONIZINGLY	PNEUMATIC	SUBVERSIVE
ODIOUS	SUBLIME	DECONDITION	PRECIPICE	ASSET

Brave New World Vocabulary

CAJOLERY	APPREHENSIVELY	PARENTHETICALLY	INGRATIATING	GESTICULATING
AXIOMATIC	ORDURE	IGNOMINY	MORIBUND	APPALLING
FLAGRANTLY	CONTEMPTUOUS	FREE SPACE	VITRIFIED	OPTIMUM
ENDORSE	COMPUNCTION	PLAINTIVE	INDEFATIGABLY	INTRINSICALLY
IMPUNITY	INCONCEIVABLE	POSTULATES	RECIPROCATED	ANNIHILATING

Brave New World Vocabulary

INDULGENTLY	BENEVOLENTLY	CAJOLERY	COMPUNCTION	ODIOUS
MONOGAMY	PARENTHETICALLY	LECHEROUS	ASSET	PRODIGIOUS
MORIBUND	RUMINATING	FREE SPACE	FLAGRANTLY	CARAPACE
IGNOMINY	IRRESOLUTE	ANNIHILATING	CHRONIC	BESTIAL
ORDURE	ENDORSE	UNABASHED	FLACCID	INEXORABLY

Brave New World Vocabulary

GESTICULATING	INDEFATIGABLY	PATRONIZINGLY	APPALLING	AXIOMATIC
SUBVERSIVE	IMPUNITY	PRECIPICE	LUMINOUS	RECIPROCATED
CASTE	UNPRECEDENTED	FREE SPACE	INTRINSICALLY	APPREHENSIVELY
VITRIFIED	SUBLIME	PLAINTIVE	PROLIFERATE	IMPERCEPTIBLY
POSTULATES	INGRATIATING	REPARATION	OPTIMUM	INCONCEIVABLE

Brave New World Vocabulary

CARAPACE	CASTE	BESTIAL	IRRESOLUTE	ORDURE
REPARATION	INEXORABLY	INGRATIATING	RUMINATING	INDULGENTLY
CAJOLERY	PROLIFERATE	FREE SPACE	CONTEMPTUOUS	LECHEROUS
BENEVOLENTLY	OPTIMUM	PNEUMATIC	INCONCEIVABLE	PLAINTIVE
PRODIGIOUS	ASSET	DECONDITION	MORIBUND	ODIOUS

Brave New World Vocabulary

FLAGRANTLY	APPALLING	AXIOMATIC	SUBLIME	SUBVERSIVE
UNPRECEDENTED	CHRONIC	IMPUNITY	UNABASHED	INSURMOUNTABLE
POSTULATES	IMPERCEPTIBLY	FREE SPACE	MONOGAMY	LUMINOUS
VITRIFIED	PATRONIZINGLY	GESTICULATING	INTRINSICALLY	PARENTHETICALLY
APPREHENSIVELY	ENDORSE	PRECIPICE	ANNIHILATING	IGNOMINY

Brave New World Vocabulary

PNEUMATIC	PATRONIZINGLY	CONTEMPTUOUS	COMPUNCTION	APPREHENSIVELY
ANNIHILATING	PRODIGIOUS	OPTIMUM	INCONCEIVABLE	UNABASHED
RUMINATING	AXIOMATIC	FREE SPACE	POSTULATES	REPARATION
UNPRECEDENTED	CAJOLERY	PARENTHETICALLY	INGRATIATING	MORIBUND
VITRIFIED	PROLIFERATE	DECONDITION	ORDURE	CASTE

Brave New World Vocabulary

SUBVERSIVE	PRECIPICE	SUBLIME	INDEFATIGABLY	ENDORSE
LECHEROUS	BESTIAL	IRRESOLUTE	INTRINSICALLY	INSURMOUNTABLE
LUMINOUS	CARAPACE	FREE SPACE	MONOGAMY	PLAINTIVE
CHRONIC	FLAGRANTLY	ODIOUS	APPALLING	INEXORABLY
INDULGENTLY	GESTICULATING	FLACCID	IMPERCEPTIBLY	RECIPROCATED

Brave New World Vocabulary

INDULGENTLY	BENEVOLENTLY	BESTIAL	ENDORSE	IMPERCEPTIBLY
GESTICULATING	CHRONIC	DECONDITION	MORIBUND	ASSET
ORDURE	INGRATIATING	FREE SPACE	AXIOMATIC	IRRESOLUTE
IGNOMINY	UNPRECEDENTED	VITRIFIED	PROLIFERATE	PATRONIZINGLY
SUBVERSIVE	MONOGAMY	PRODIGIOUS	CASTE	APPREHENSIVELY

Brave New World Vocabulary

UNABASHED	OPTIMUM	COMPUNCTION	INEXORABLY	CARAPACE
ODIOUS	PRECIPICE	INDEFATIGABLY	FLACCID	SUBLIME
CAJOLERY	IMPUNITY	FREE SPACE	POSTULATES	PARENTHETICALLY
ANNIHILATING	INSURMOUNTABLE	PNEUMATIC	INCONCEIVABLE	REPARATION
CONTEMPTUOUS	APPALLING	RECIPROCATED	PLAINTIVE	INTRINSICALLY

Brave New World Vocabulary

LECHEROUS	FLAGRANTLY	DECONDITION	RECIPROCATED	UNPRECEDENTED
POSTULATES	PROLIFERATE	ENDORSE	ODIOUS	REPARATION
BENEVOLENTLY	SUBLIME	FREE SPACE	ORDURE	IRRESOLUTE
UNABASHED	IMPERCEPTIBLY	RUMINATING	CAJOLERY	PRECIPICE
PRODIGIOUS	VITRIFIED	PATRONIZINGLY	INSURMOUNTABLE	BESTIAL

Brave New World Vocabulary

OPTIMUM	FLACCID	COMPUNCTION	INCONCEIVABLE	LUMINOUS
INDEFATIGABLY	CARAPACE	INDULGENTLY	ANNIHILATING	IMPUNITY
PNEUMATIC	MORIBUND	FREE SPACE	AXIOMATIC	SUBVERSIVE
INEXORABLY	CASTE	MONOGAMY	PARENTHETICALLY	APPREHENSIVELY
IGNOMINY	APPALLING	INGRATIATING	CHRONIC	PLAINTIVE

www.ingramcontent.com/pod-product-compliance
Lightning Source LLC
Chambersburg PA
CBHW081455070526
44586CB00019B/2371